SPRINKLES!

Sprinkles!

Recipes and Ideas for Rainbowlicious Desserts

By Jackie Alpers

© 2013 by Quirk Productions, Inc.

Library of Congress Cataloging in Publication Number: 2012953944
ISBN: 978-1-59474-638-3
Printed in China
Typeset in Bodoni, Futura
Designed by Sugar
Art direction by Katie Hatz
Photography by Jackie Alpers, unless otherwise noted
Photography on page 110 by Kelsey McClellan, resident photographer at Jeni's Splendid Ice Creams
Prop styling: Rosy Strazzeri-Fridman
Food styling: Danielle Westberg
Production management by John J. McGurk

The Darkest Chocolate Ice Cream in the World on pages 110–112 excerpted with permission from
Jeni's Splendid Ice Creams at Home by Jeni Britton Bauer (Artisan Books, 2011).

The Tropical Pearl Cocktail on page 127 is based on a recipe contributed by Warren Bobrow,
cocktail whisperer and author of *Apothecary Cocktails: Restorative Drinks from Yesterday and Today*
(Quayside Books, 2013).

The Rainbow Layer Cake on the cover and pages 72–75 appears courtesy of Maribel Cervantes.

Quirk Books
215 Church St.
Philadelphia, PA 19106
quirkbooks.com
10 9 8 7 6 5 4 3 2 1

HAPPINESS IS RAINBOW SPRINKLES

Contents

Hi there!

I am so happy to be bringing you a book called *Sprinkles!* How could I not be? Sprinkles are all about delight—with their color, sweetness, and little bit of crunch, they bring a visible layer of joy to everything they adorn. Sprinkles make the world a better, more rainbowlicious place. They exist, pure and simple, to make happiness.

But the world of sprinkles is far from simple. From the nearly microscopic to the size of a peanut, the term sprinkle encompasses all things cute and sweet, in every shape you can imagine. The power of sprinkles is anything but superficial. Whether it's a host of multicolored sequins showered on a slice of fairy bread or one perfectly placed dragée topping off a cupcake, a sprinkly sheen on a sweet treat can change everything. And the best part is, you don't have to be a pastry chef to play with sprinkles. With a few of the fun tricks in this book up your sleeve, you'll be whipping up sprinkle-studded goodies in no time.

This book is all about using the beauty of sprinkles to unleash your creativity. The recipes and how-tos are also great for kids and families who want to cook together. But above all, *Sprinkles!* is a true community effort. We saw the amazing ways that people use sprinkles, and then we incorporated some of those ideas into this book. But we'd love to see more!

We've given you the tools, knowledge, and inspiration to create your own sprinkle-tastic vision, and now it's up to you to bring it to life. The recipes are a guide, a way to illustrate all the wonderful ways to use sprinkles, but there's always room for new ideas. Let's get started and discover the rainbowlicious world of sprinkles together!

The World of Sprinkles

The sprinkles of my youth were the classics. Tiny, colorful little beads of rainbow nonpareils on a chocolate-dipped cone on a summer afternoon. Edible silver BB's circling the base of a smooth white cake. Even the chocolate jimmies I scooped up by the handful and poured into my mouth before getting caught. (Sorry, Mom. It was worth it!) But times have changed. Thanks to today's cupcake-crazed society, a vast world of sprinkles has emerged. Here's a guide to identifying and baking with them, from the classic to the exotic.

Sprinkles: These are small bits of confectionery whose sole purpose is to add texture, decoration, and fun to baked goods and sweets. The generic term *sprinkles* usually refers to the ball- or rod-shaped opaque sugar pieces, whereas the word *décoratif* can refer to anything that decorates the surface of a sweet. Sprinkles are typically manufactured using the extrusion method, in which a sugar-starch mixture is squeezed through tiny holes into long strands. The strands are then tossed in a circular or oval pan mounted on an angled, spinning post to break them into small pieces called *vermicelli* (literally "little worms"). After a glaze of a light sugar syrup, the batch of sprinkles is sifted to remove oversized bits and then reglazed to add a little extra shine and crunch.

Jimmies: This American term for sprinkles was coined around the 1920s and refers only to the rod-shaped sprinkles, and sometimes specifically to chocolate ones, depending on whom you ask. Like traditional sprinkles, jimmies are typically manufactured using the extrusion method (see above).

Hagelslag (literally "hailstorm"): A Dutch variety of sprinkle popular for breakfast, traditionally made with chocolate but now available in vanilla and fruit flavors.

Nonpareils: The French name (literally "not equal") shows just how indispensable pastry chefs find these minuscule ball-shaped bits of sugar and starch. Nonpareils are traditionally made in opaque white, but these days they're available in single- or multicolored mixes. (The name is also used for a chocolate drop candy that's made with these sweet tiny beads; for the recipe, see page 124.)

Hundreds and Thousands: An alternate name for sprinkles in the United Kingdom, Australia, and New Zealand, hundreds and thousands usually refers to the round, multicolored sort (see "Nonpareils").

Dragées: In French, *dragée* refers specifically to a sugar-coated almond, but the term in English means any kind of small confectionery with a hard shell made by panning an edible center in candy coating.

Panned Chocolate: Small disks of chocolate are coated with a candy shell (this technology was invented by the U.S. military for easier transport of chocolate!). Think M&Ms and Smarties. Though most people love to eat these sweets on their own, many brands come in a variety of sizes for decorating.

Sixlets: These are larger (about 10 millimeters in diameter) candy-covered chocolate-flavored balls that come in a variety of colors and are available in matte or pearl finish.

Metallic Dragées: These elegant little sugar spheres, about 3 to 4 millimeters in diameter, are coated in a shiny finish (traditionally silver) for extra gleam. Though their silver coloring no longer contains mercury (as it did in the early 1900s), the U.S. Food and Drug Administration considers these to be inedible and "for decoration only"; however, other countries, like the United Kingdom, classify them as food items. Use your own best judgment.

Jordan (Sugared) Almonds: These are almonds that have been sugar-panned in syrup that forms into a pastel-colored shell when dry. In Italy, the treats are known as confetti and color-coded for different celebrations. In Belgium, the equivalent *suikerboon* (sugar bean) is symbolic of baptism and fertility, and Greeks eat *koufeta* as wedding favors. To make a quick and easy homemade variety, try the recipe on page 135.

Liebesperlen: Translated as "love beads," this large-format sprinkle, usually about a few millimeters in diameter, is popular at German fairs, at folk festivals, and in packaged toys.

Comfits: These are dried fruits, nuts, seeds, or spices coated with sugar, traditionally given as gifts at baptisms and weddings.

Candy-Covered Anise Seeds: called muisjes ("little mice") in Dutch and traditionally eaten on a rusk biscuit after the birth of a child (they're thought to encourage lactation). **Licorice Comfits**, also called torpedoes because of their shapes. **Fruit and Seed Comfits**, including citrus, fennel, caraway, and ginger.

Pearls: As the name suggests, these are round sprinkles that have a pearlescent shine (not to be confused with pearl sugar; see page 13).

Luster Pearls: These have a glossy opalescent finish.

Sugar Pearls: These have either a matte finish or a pearl finish.

Glitters: All that glitters is not gold—sometimes, it's a sprinkle. These edible versions of the crafting staple lend a lustrous sparkle to whatever they touch.

Edible Glitter: Flakier than sparkling sugar. Metallics and various metallic colors. Comes in flakes as well as fun shapes like stars, hearts, and more.

Fine Edible Glitter: Also sold as **Disco Dust**, this is very fine glitter dust.

Luster Dust a.k.a. Pearl Dust: When mixed with a clear spirit like vodka, luster dust can be painted on a food surface for a pearly finish.

Spray-On Glitter: Available in the sprinkles section of most supermarkets, this novelty product is lots of fun. It is also known as **Edible Spray Paint**.

Confetti: Much like their nonedible namesake, these sprinkles are flat and usually colorful. Cut from sheets of tinted sugar, confetti is larger, flatter, and crunchier than the typical round sprinkle. Also known as sequins or quins. Not to be confused with Italian confetti (see above).

Jumbo Quins: Larger confetti, usually 5 millimeters and up in diameter.

Specialty Shapes: Hearts, flowers, stars, snowflakes, ghosts, and animals, oh my! Any occasion that merits a baked good can also get its own sprinkle shape.

Sugars: Unlike sprinkles, which are cooked and formed into balls, rods, or other shapes, decorative sugars are ordinary sugar crystals that have been dyed or painted for a sweet appearance. Even everyday baking or cooking sugars can add a dash of drama to your confections.

Sanding Sugars: These colored sugars get their name from the "sandy" texture of their crystals, which are square and slightly larger than those of typical granulated sugar.

Sparkling (Crystal) Sugars: A cousin to sanding sugars, these are larger sugar grains coated with a metallic or glittering finish.

Granulated (White) Sugar: The all-star cooking and baking sugar, with medium-sized crystals and a pure, sweet taste. Decorative commercial varieties include metallics like **Gold Sugar**.

Confectioners' Sugar (Powdered Sugar, Icing Sugar): Created by grinding granulated sugar into pieces of varying fineness (degrees range from XXX to 10X—the more Xs, the finer the sugar) and is often used to dust the tops of cakes or make smooth icings and glazes.

Superfine (Caster) Sugar: This has a specific grade of fineness: larger than most confectioners' sugar, but about half that of granulated sugar.

Brown Sugar: This is granulated sugar given a rich color and flavor from the presence of molasses, which is either left in during sugarcane processing or added back to white sugar. Dark brown sugar has a molasses content of 6.5 percent, while light brown sugar has 3.5 percent. Natural brown sugar is brown sugar made from the first processing of sugar cane: the less it is processed, the higher the molasses content.

Muscovado Sugar: This is the darkest of the bunch, taking its name from the Spanish *más abacado*, meaning "more finished" than molasses.

Turbinado Sugar: This is made by crystallizing raw sugar cane juice and has lighter-colored, less sticky granules than other brown sugars. **Demerara Sugar** is made in the same process, but has a lower molasses content than light brown sugar.

Pearl Sugar: Coarse, large, and shaped like little pearls, this sugar is made either by crushing blocks of white sugar or by pushing sugar through an extrusion die. The resulting crystals do not melt at typical oven temperatures and are used to decorate the tops of baked goods. In Scandinavia, *perlesukker* is found on pastries like Finnish *pulla*, Swedish *bulle*, and *kanelbullar* (cinnamon buns). Belgian baking favors it for its famous Liège waffles, and French brioche will often include a sprinkling of the pearls on top.

Rock Sugar: With crystals larger than both granulated and sanding sugar, rock sugar resembles broken-up rock candy and comes in a variety of colors.

Flavored Sugars: These are usually made by steeping, rubbing, or mixing a flavored ingredient with granulated sugar. See page 134 for how to make your own **Vanilla Sugar, Cinnamon Sugar, Herb Sugar,** and **Citrus Sugar**. Commercial varieties are available.

Chocolate Bits: Sweets without chocolate are practically unthinkable! Fortunately, you're spoiled for choice: from cocoa powder to curls and chips, almost every form of the fruit of the cacao tree can become sprinkle-friendly.

Cocoa Powder: The powdered product made from the remains left after cocoa butter is extracted. Many commercial powders are Dutch-process cocoa, which is treated with an alkalizing agent for a smoother flavor, but natural cocoa may also be found.

Cocoa Nibs: Cocoa beans that have been roasted and winnowed to remove their husks, with a nutty, coffeelike flavor. They are not sweet, so you'll want to pair them with a sweet or savory topping for depth of flavor.

Chocolate Shavings and Curls: Dainty peels of chocolate made using a peeler to scrape bits off a slightly softened bar of chocolate.

Chocolate Chips: Small chunks of chocolate with a flat-bottom teardrop shape. Larger pieces come in chunks, and smaller ones may be sold as **morsels** or **mini morsels**.

Fancy Salts: Don't shy away from salt! A small pinch of salt on top of everything from caramels to cupcakes will give treats an unexpected boost of flavor (not saltiness). The best sprinkling salts are natural, uniodized salts that lend a clean flavor and fresh edge to whatever they land on, sweet or savory.

Sea Salt: Sold in flakes or crystals, these refined salts are harvested from waters worldwide, most notably from France, Sicily, and England. **Fleur de sel** (literally "flower of salt") refers to flaky French sea salt, slightly gray and moist from its mineral composition. **Maldon salt** is a popular brand harvested in Maldon, England, that has light flakes and crunchy texture.

Pink (Himalayan) Rock Salt: Mined in the Khewra Salt Mines of Pakistan, this salt's reddish-pink hue makes it a favorite for decorating.

Lay-Ons: As their name suggests, these larger, shaped décoratifs are made for purposeful placing rather than scattering. Lay-ons are formed by pressing tinted sugar into molds, yielding one side shaped like anything from a bumblebee to a baseball and another, flat side for easy adherence.

Crushed Goodies: A rustic, homemade batch of sprinkles is just a few thumps away! Just put your favorite breakable treats or candies in a plastic bag, cover with a dishtowel, and roll or crunch with a rolling pin. Good options include peppermints and candy canes, vanilla wafers, chocolate cookies, pretzels, and graham crackers.

Solid-Color Candies: Even though they're made for standalone snacking, these smaller-than-bite-size candies are great for sprinkling and lend a new kind of flavor and crunch to your creations. Try Nerds, Tic Tacs, Gumballs, Mini Malt Balls, Runts, candy dots, and jelly beans (the particularly small and flavorful Jelly Bellies are a good choice).

Batter Bits: Wilton's **ColorBurst Batter Bits** are bright bursts of edible color that can be swirled into cake batter or other baked goods. When baked, these corn-cereal-based bits soften with moisture but do not lose their color or shape—they just develop a rich, cakey texture when they come out of the oven.

Crunches and Crumbles: Available in a variety of flavors such as cookie cream, orange cream, cotton candy, and nut crunch, these packaged toppings add loads of color, texture, and much more flavor than your standard sprinkles. Dean Jacob's **Ice Cream Crunch** is great for ice cream, sure, but it's also a good match for Nutella or cookie butter (as on page 42).

Know Your Sprinkles!

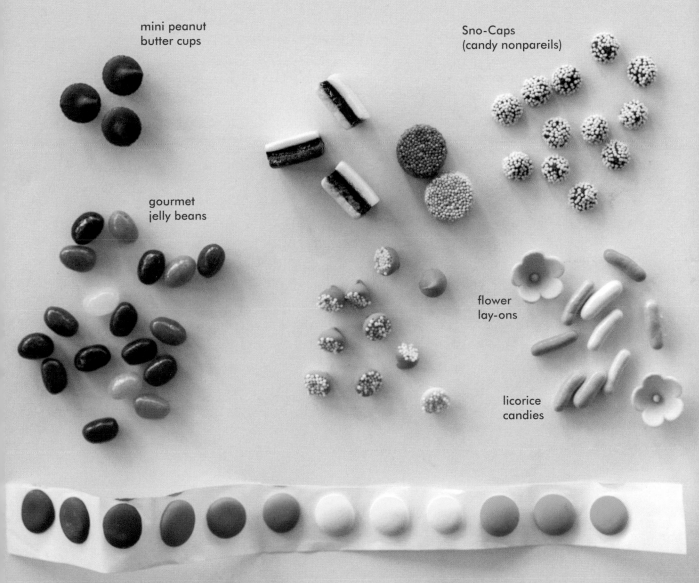

mini peanut
butter cups

Sno-Caps
(candy nonpareils)

gourmet
jelly beans

flower
lay-ons

licorice
candies

candy dots

Pick your palette.

dark blue and light
blue jimmies with white
snowflake-shaped
confetti

star-shaped confetti
in assorted colors

black, white, and brown
cow-shaped confetti

quins in assorted
colors (often called
"carnival" colors)

jumbo quins (a.k.a. sequins)
in assorted colors

heart-shaped
confetti

mini heart-shaped
confetti

diamond confetti in
assorted colors

raspberry red-colored
sanding sugar

Belgian pearl sugar

natural turbinado sugar

crystal sugar

rock sugar

confectioners' sugar

fleur de sel

chocolate candy melt

chocolate
chips

chocolate-
covered coffee
beans

pink (Himalayan)
rock salt

chocolate bar
chunks

cocoa nibs

Let's get colorful!

white nonpareils

metallic dragées

sixlets

candy beads in
assorted colors

black sugar pearls

rainbow nonpareils

luster pearls and sugar
pearls in assorted colors

edible glitter
in metallic
colors: aqua,
pink, white,
yellow, and
purple

Put some sparkle in
your sweets.

copper edible glitter

gold sugar

silver luster dust
(a.k.a. pearl dust)

gold edible glitter

silver sugar

Sprinkling Methods

Everybody loves sprinkles on top—but everybody's also got a different way of getting them there. Are you the type of person who likes to hold your hands way up in the air and drop sprinkles from a height for even distribution? Or are you the type who likes to meticulously place tiny hearts one by one to cover the surface of a cake? Or maybe you break the mold with sprinkles ice cubes for party beverages? Try these methods on for size, and see what sticks!

SPRINKLE!

for a casual look. The idea here is to let the pieces fall where they may. Sprinkling is inherently random (if you want to control your sprinkles, see **Arrange**, page 22), and the best way to sprinkle is to do it with abandon. Let chaos prevail. Grab a pinch (or a handful!) of sprinkles, hold them at least 6 inches above the surface you want to cover, and let gravity do the rest.

DUST!

with fine glitter or smaller sprinkles for a glamorous look. Use a shaker to avoid clumping, and do the dusting right before serving for best results (the moisture in baked goods can dissolve fine sugars). If you want to make shapes or sharper lines using dust, see **Stencil** (page 23).

SWIRL!

into batter, frosting, or whipped cream. Nonpareils and dragées are your best bet for this method, since they tend to keep their color and shape even after being mixed in. When in doubt, test first, but remember, dissolving is sometimes a good thing—the confetti cake craze was born when someone noticed that jimmies dissolve in baked goods and leave behind those lovely colored spots. Either way, it's a good idea to test the sprinkles on a small portion of a recipe: some brands of sprinkles hold their color better than others, so you'll want to make sure you're getting the desired effect.

DIP, DUNK, AND COAT!

tops of cupcakes, pretzel rods, candy sticks, pieces of fruit, marshmallow kabobs…the possibilities are endless. If a treat can be dipped or dunked in chocolate or candy melts, it can also be coated with sprinkles. Lighter-weight sprinkles (like sanding sugar or glitter) will stick best, but don't let that stop you from exploring! Go wild and have fun—everything's better with a colorful candy coating.

EDGE!

the sides of whoopie pies, cookies, cakes, and the like. Who would choose a plain ol' cookie over one edged in sprinkles? NO ONE. Pretty to the eye equals tastier in the belly—it's a scientific fact. And a little extra crunch doesn't hurt, either!

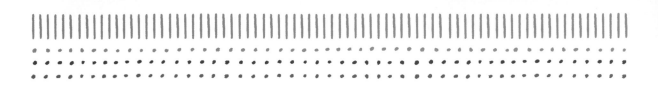

ARRANGE!

one by one in a pretty pattern, design, or lettering—you can use kitchen tweezers or go freehand. All you need is a steady hand and sprinkles that have a decent amount of surface area (save your fine dusts and glitters for another time). If you want to rearrange every sprinkle that so that it is placed just so, this is your chance—make something as simple as a short message or as deluxe as a whole mosaic.

Part of the fun of using sprinkles in the kitchen is lavishly adorning your confections with utter abandon. But sometimes a single perfectly placed quin is just what a dish needs to go from just pretty to spectacular. On those occasions, kitchen tweezers can save the day. (See "Sprinkles Sources," page 136, for where you can buy a good pair for this purpose.) This handy tool allows you to achieve a dainty design that looks like it took much longer to create than it really did— and you won't muss up frostings with your fingertips or spill sprinkles anywhere but where you want them.

STRIPE!

multiple types or colors onto frosting or other sticky surface. Striping can be done either freehand or with a stencil (or strip of wax paper) and isn't limited to straight lines—try cutting out waves or zigzags!

MIX & LAYER!

multiple types, colors mixed together, or a whole bunch of shapes and shades on top of one another. What's better than sprinkles? MORE SPRINKLES! Plan a matching set of sprinkles by color (a bunch of blues) or shape (all kinds of little hearts) or abandon plans altogether and go crazy with a mishmash!

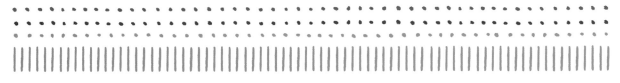

SUSPEND!

in solid treats like lollipops, popsicles, and ice cubes. Since you want your bits and pieces to stay intact and spread out, not dissolve or sink to the bottom, the sprinkles you use should be sturdy but not heavier than the mixture you're suspending them in. It may take a few tries to get it right, but don't worry—mistakes taste just as good.

STENCIL!

cookies, cakes, and other flat surfaces. Stenciling is basically controlled dusting: apply sprinkles through doilies, cookie cutters, or kitchen utensils like spatulas for easy, graphic looks. For a guide to stenciling see page 68.

GLITTER & GLUE!

with an old-school technique. I remember sitting by myself on the living room floor, armed with the standard-issue childhood art supplies: a sheet of navy blue construction paper, a bottle of Elmer's white glue, and a baby food jar half filled with silver glitter. I'd carefully squeeze the glue onto the paper, spelling out my name. That was the hard part, the meticulous part. Next came the easy part. I took all the glitter and dumped it on top of the glue in one big clump. Then I waited. The glue dried. I shook off the excess glitter, and voilà! Art!

You can use this same technique to decorate cookies. All you have to do is replace the glue for a squeeze bottle filled with frosting and make the glitter the edible kind. Small nonpareils will also work; larger sprinkles and jimmies tend to fall off. Squeeze bottles, pastry bags with small tips (such as #2), and condiment pens all work well for glitter-and-glue styling. See "Sprinkles Sources" (page 136) for where to find them.

Breakfast Sweets

Plenty of classic breakfast foods come studded with sprinkles—but why stop there? Whip up Fancified Doughnuts, Belgian Pearl Sugar Waffles, and Homemade Pop Tarts to give the usual suspects a wink and a smile. Or try twinkly new twists on old favorites like Sprinkles-Stuffed French Toast or Happy Day Pancakes with Sparkling Syrup. Top it all off with a glittering glass of sangria and you'll discover a whole new meaning of "rise and shine."

in Belgium, they're just called waffles

❖ Belgian Pearl Sugar Waffles ❖

MAKES 4 TO 6 LARGE WAFFLES

The heat of a waffle iron will burn most sprinkles that are mixed into waffle batter, leaving a gooey mess. In Belgium, a fluffy, delicious confection known as the Liège waffle or "sugar waffle" has sturdy pearl sugar mixed into the batter, which caramelizes on the outside instead of burning.

WAFFLES
1 tablespoon packed light brown sugar
1½ teaspoons active dry yeast
2 cups all-purpose flour
½ teaspoon salt
2 large eggs, at room temperature
½ cup (1 stick) unsalted butter, plus additional melted butter for cooking
1 teaspoon pure vanilla extract
½ cup Belgian pearl sugar*

TOPPING
2 tablespoons confectioners' sugar
1 teaspoon ground cinnamon
A few teaspoons white snowflake confetti sprinkles, optional
Sprinkles Whipped Cream (page 41), optional

Swedish pearl sugar and most other sugar nibs can be substituted, but they may be smaller than the Belgian type. (See page 13 for more on the differences between pearl sugars.)

1 In a small bowl, whisk brown sugar and yeast into ¼ cup lukewarm water and let stand until foamy, about 5 minutes. In a large bowl combine flour and salt; make a well in the center and pour in the yeast mixture. With an electric mixer on medium speed, beat for 1 minute. Add eggs one at a time, mixing for 20 seconds after each addition.

2 Lower mixer speed to medium-low and gradually mix in butter and vanilla, beating until smooth; the batter will be thick and sticky. Cover the bowl with plastic wrap and let the batter rise in a warm place until doubled in size, about 1 hour and 45 minutes.

3 Gently fold pearl sugar into the risen batter. Cover again and let rest for 15 minutes. Preheat a Belgian waffle iron and brush it with melted butter. Gently stir the batter to deflate.

4 Using about ½ to ¾ cup batter for each, cook waffles according to the manufacturer's directions until golden and crisp; brush the waffle iron with melted butter as needed. Transfer waffles to plates or place them in a warm oven until ready to serve.

5 To serve, sprinkle waffles with confectioners' sugar, cinnamon, more pearl sugar, and confetti sprinkles. Top with a cloud of Sprinkles Whipped Cream, if desired.

Belgian waffles are made with yeast instead of baking powder, so allow a couple hours for them to rise. Often served at street fairs, they are perfect for breakfast any time of the day.

start the day off right

Happy Day Pancakes

MAKES 4

Fluffy buttermilk pancakes can't get any better—
unless you add sprinkles!

2 cups all-purpose flour

3 tablespoons sugar

½ teaspoon salt

1 teaspoon baking powder

½ teaspoon baking soda

1½ cups buttermilk

2 eggs, beaten

¼ cup (½ stick) unsalted butter, melted and cooled

1 teaspoon pure vanilla extract

3 tablespoons confetti sprinkles, in shades of blue or other colors

1 Whisk together flour, sugar, salt, baking powder, and baking soda in a large bowl. In a second large bowl, whisk together buttermilk, eggs, melted butter, and vanilla. Make a well in the center of the dry ingredients and pour in wet ingredients. Stir until well combined but still a little lumpy.

2 For each pancake, spoon about ¼ cup batter onto a hot griddle or skillet coated with cooking spray. Add sprinkles. Flip pancake when the edges look dry and the bubbles that have formed on the surface start to break. Cook for 1 to 2 minutes longer, or until completely golden brown.

HOW AND WHEN TO ADD SPRINKLES

Pancakes are cooked at a fairly low temperature, so it's fine to mix sprinkles into the batter. Because the batter's wetness may dissolve them bit, scatter another layer right before flipping the pancakes so that the sprinkles really stand out on the surface.

Top your sprinkly pancakes, waffles, or French toast with sprinkles compound butter (page 36) and sprinkles syrup (page 37). Sprinkles on sprinkles on sprinkles!

Sparkling Syrup

MAKES 2 CUPS

This light and easy-to-prepare syrup is delicious over pancakes,
waffles, or ice cream. Tinted with color from fresh fruit,
it's an incredibly tasty vehicle for your favorite sprinkles.

½ cup sugar

½ cup fresh or frozen fruit,
such as strawberries, blueberries,
raspberries, or sliced peaches

3 tablespoons sprinkles
of your choice

1 In a small saucepan over medium heat, bring 2 cups water, sugar, and fruit to a simmer.

2 Cook for 4 minutes. Pour mixture through a fine-mesh strainer into a clean heatproof container with a lid. Discard solids. Cover and let cool. Once syrup is completely cool, stir in sprinkles. Refrigerate for up to 1 month.

LOADS OF FLAVORS

Sprinkles suspended in simple syrup or maple syrup hold their shape well. Just remember not to heat the syrup to avoid melting the sprinkles. Here are a couple from-scratch recipes to get you started.

Rainbow Sprinkles Maple Syrup: Gradually, to avoid clumping, stir 3 tablespoons sprinkles into 1 cup pure maple syrup. Pour into a clean jar with a lid, seal, and store in the refrigerator for up to 3 months. *Makes 1 cup*

Decadent Chocolate Syrup: Because of its rich dark color, this syrup is best dotted with sprinkles on top, not stirred in, just before serving. Heat 1 tablespoon butter in a cast-iron skillet over medium-low heat. Mix in ½ cup sugar and ½ cup unsweetened cocoa powder. Slowly pour in ½ cup water and whisk well to break up lumps. Whisk in ¼ teaspoon salt. Simmer for 3 to 4 minutes, stirring occasionally. The syrup will thicken as it cools.

over-the-top highfalutin coffee dunkers

⋯❖ Fancified Doughnuts ❖⋯

MAKES ABOUT 20 DOUGHNUTS

A fat, warm, homemade doughnut with glaze dripping down the sides beats
the store-bought variety any day. For a quicker alternative, skip the doughnut
cutter and simply roll dough into 2-inch balls, ready for frying.

DOUGHNUTS

2 cups all-purpose flour

½ cup sugar

¼ teaspoon salt

4 teaspoons baking powder

½ teaspoon ground cinnamon

Pinch freshly grated nutmeg

½ cup milk

2 teaspoons unsalted butter,
melted and cooled

1 egg, beaten

About 3 cups vegetable oil, such
as canola, for frying*

TOPPING

2 cups All-Purpose Glaze
(page 32), tinted pink (or the
color of your choice)

⅓ cup small yellow nonpareils or
sprinkles of your choice

*About 3 cups, depending
on the size of your pot.*

1 In a medium bowl, whisk to combine flour, sugar, salt, baking powder, cinnamon, and nutmeg. In another bowl, add milk and butter to egg and whisk to combine. By hand or with an electric mixer on medium-low speed, beat flour mixture into egg mixture.

2 On a lightly floured surface, gently knead the dough. Roll out dough to about ¼ inch thick. Using a doughnut cutter or two circle cookie cutters (one small, one large), cut out doughnuts. Roll scraps into 2-inch balls.

3 Line a baking sheet or drying rack with paper towels. Fill a large, heavy-bottom pot with oil to a depth of 2 to 3 inches. Over medium-high heat, bring oil to 375°F.

4 Gently lower doughnuts into the hot oil in batches of 2 or 3 to keep them from colliding; turn them over as they rise to the surface. Fry until they're golden brown, about 1 minute per side. Transfer doughnuts to the baking sheet to drain and cool.

5 Spoon glaze over cooled doughnuts. Sprinkle nonpareils over top. Let glaze set for about 10 minutes before serving.

MORE TO TRY

Cinnamon-Sugar Munchkins: Instead of glazing, roll fresh doughnut holes in Cinnamon Sugar (page 134) to coat.

Rainbow-Filled Munchkins: Load Sprinkles Pastry Cream (page 95) into a piping bag fitted with a metal tip. When doughnuts are cool, insert the tip into each one and squeeze in about 1 tablespoon of filling. Top filled munchkins with glaze and sprinkles or roll in sanding sugar to coat.

gets those sprinkles to stay put!

All-Purpose Glaze

MAKES 2 CUPS

Sprinkles lovers, meet your new best friend! When you want these tiny confections to stick to your treats, glaze is the secret weapon. This recipe can be tinted any color—it's as adaptable as it is delicious.

1½ cups confectioners' sugar

½ teaspoon pure vanilla extract

¼ teaspoon almond extract, optional

⅛ teaspoon salt

2 to 3 tablespoons whole milk

1 tablespoon butter, very soft

A few drops food coloring, optional

1 Whisk together confectioners' sugar, vanilla extract, almond extract (if using), and salt. Add 2 tablespoons milk and whisk to blend, adding the additional tablespoon as needed to create a shiny, pourable glaze.

2 Whisk in butter until incorporated. Stir in food coloring if using. Use immediately or store, refrigerated in an airtight container, for up to 1 week.

Doughnuts and sprinkles are a classic combination. But that doesn't mean your decorated doughnuts need to be boring. Experiment with different colors of glazes and sprinkles to come up with your own unique mix-and-match treat.

the breakfast classic goes glam

❖ Sprinkles-Stuffed French Toast ❖

MAKES 2 STUFFED TOASTS

What's better than French toast for breakfast? Why, French toast stuffed with sprinkles and sugar and spice and everything nice, of course! This recipe couldn't be easier—just adjust the amounts of vanilla and cinnamon to taste.

4 eggs*

¼ cup milk or cream

1 teaspoon ground cinnamon

¼ cup sprinkles, any color

1 tablespoon pure vanilla extract

4 thick slices bread**

¼ cup cream cheese

¼ cup apricot or berry jam

¼ cup sprinkles***

2 tablespoons pure maple syrup

*Or 1 cup egg substitute.

**I like to use hearty bread; the thicker the slices, the better they soak up the egg mixture. For a sweet alternative, try banana bread or pound cake.

***Any type of sprinkles will do, but I like to use Wilton's ColorBurst Batter Bits for their soft flecks of color. They hold their form throughout the cooking process.

1 Whisk together eggs, milk, cinnamon, sprinkles, and vanilla until frothy. Soak bread in egg mixture for 10 seconds on each side.

2 Coat a large skillet with cooking spray and place over medium-low heat. Add soaked bread to skillet and cook for about 4 minutes on each side, or until golden brown. Remove skillet from heat, cover, and let rest for 2 minutes.

3 Spread 2 pieces of French toast with a layer of cream cheese and a layer of jam. Top each with another piece of French toast to make two sandwiches. Or continue layering fillings and French toast to make one big stack.

Letting hot French toast rest for a minute or two before serving makes it fluffier and even more delicious.

FOR CHOCOLATE LOVERS

Chocolate Sprinkles Stuffed French Toast: Omit jam and replace the cream cheese with chocolate hazelnut spread. Use chocolate sprinkles if desired.

a quick and easy spread

⁘ I ♥ Sprinkles Butter ⁘

MAKES 1 CUP

Mix up your very own sprinkles butter and refrigerate or freeze it for later. A pat on toast is enough to brighten anybody's morning. It's also perfect with French toast and waffles (as on pages 35 and 27) or other sweet-and-savory delights.

1 cup (2 sticks) salted or unsalted butter,* at room temperature

¼ cup colored jimmies or other multicolored sprinkles of your choice

2 tablespoons honey

For a balanced sweet and savory flavor, I like to use a good-quality salted butter, such as Kerrygold.

1 By hand or with an electric mixer on low speed, beat butter until smooth and then mix in jimmies or sprinkles. Stir in honey.

2 Spoon sprinkles butter into a sealable airtight container and refrigerate for up to 1 month.

A compound butter is any butter that is mixed with sprinkles, sugar, fancy salt, herbs, or other mix-ins and then reshaped into a log or scooped into a jar for later use. The longer a compound butter sits, the more the mix-ins impart flavor (and, in some cases, aroma) to the butter. Compound butter will keep in refrigerator for up to 1 month.

MORE TO TRY

Fruity Sprinkles Butter: Mix in 1 tablespoon dried fruit, such as apricots, along with the honey.

Fancy Salt and Herb Butter: Dried herbs and fancy salts—like the ones on page 14—make for a lovely savory version of this easily adaptable recipe. Use about ½ teaspoon of salt and ¼ cup of herbs per 2 sticks of butter and omit the honey.

a happy snack-time treat

❖ Fairy Bread Sandwiches ❖

MAKES 4 SANDWICHES

Inspired by Robert Louis Stevenson's poem "Fairy Bread" in
A Child's Garden of Verses, this treat is popular at children's parties in Australia,
New Zealand, and other parts of the world.

About 2 tablespoons unsalted butter,* at room temperature

8 slices bread

About ½ cup nonpareils, jimmies, confetti, or sparkling sugar

Butter is typically used, but cream cheese, jam, Nutella, and Gingersnap Cookie Butter (page 42) are also suitable for catching sprinkles.

1 Spread a thin layer of butter on one side of each slice of bread. Use cookie cutters to cut out shapes from 4 of the buttered slices.

2 Place the uncut slices, buttered side up, on a plate or over a bowl to catch excess sprinkles. Cover with sprinkles. Top with the cut-out slices, buttered side down.

Just barely sweet, these sandwiches make a fun breakfast surprise, after-school snack, or party food.

Fudge Puppies

MAKES 24

Covered in chocolate, whipped cream, and all your favorite toppings,
fudge puppies are a staple at state fairs. I like to make them miniature and serve
them in cupcake wrappers at parties, picnics, and get-togethers.

6 Belgian waffles or 24 mini waffles*

8 to 16 ounces chocolate**

½ cup rainbow sprinkles, nonpareils, dragées, or a combination

½ cup crushed peanuts, optional

Whipped cream or Sprinkles Whipped Cream (page 41), for topping

6 maraschino cherries or large candies, for topping

For a homemade recipe, see page 27. Store-bought frozen waffles work just as well!

**Almost any dark, milk, or even white chocolate will work in this recipe. It's better to melt too much chocolate than not enough, because when you melt a small amount it's more likely to burn and become unusable.*

1 Toast waffles. If using Belgian waffles, cut each into 4 equal squares.

2 Melt chocolate in the microwave or a glass or metal bowl set over a pot of simmering water, stirring frequently.

3 Line a work surface with parchment paper. Using a fork or tongs, dip each waffle in chocolate to coat in a smooth, even layer. Then dip it in sprinkles, peanuts, or other assorted toppings. Place on parchment paper to cool and set.

4 Transfer cooled fudge puppies to cupcake wrappers. Top with whipped cream and more sprinkles and nuts, if desired. Decorate each with a maraschino cherry or a piece of candy on top.

STICK 'EM UP

To serve these treats on sticks, insert skewers into the waffles after cutting them into squares. Place them on a baking sheet, cover, and freeze for about 30 minutes. (This helps the waffles stay on their sticks.) Remove them from the freezer when you're ready to dip and decorate.

poufy clouds of edible sparkles

Sprinkles Whipped Cream

MAKES 4 CUPS

Just think how a pretty homemade whipped cream
will dress up your party.

2 cups very cold heavy cream

½ teaspoon pure vanilla extract

¼ cup confectioners' sugar

A few drops food coloring, optional

1 tablespoon to 1 cup sprinkles,* to taste

Jimmies, confetti, nonpareils—most small to medium sprinkles work well in this recipe. They just have to be colorful and substantial enough not to disappear in the folds of whipped cream.

1 In a large mixing bowl, combine heavy cream, vanilla, and confectioners' sugar. Refrigerate for at least 30 minutes.

2 Using an electric mixer fitted with the whisk attachment, whip mixture on high speed for 3 minutes, or until it forms soft, billowy peaks. Use a rubber spatula to gently fold in sprinkles. Serve or refrigerate for up to 3 hours.

possibly the most magical thing in the world

·❖· Gingersnap Cookie Butter ·❖·

MAKES 1 CUP

Also known as speculoos butter, cookie butter was dreamed up by modern-day Belgian chefs looking to create a spreadable version of a traditional Belgian cookie. It's an irresistible concoction that has become an international sensation. In this version, crispy gingersnap cookies replace the usual windmill variety as the main ingredient.

6 ounces (about 16 small) crisp gingersnap cookies

1 tablespoon packed brown sugar

1 tablespoon ground cinnamon

1 teaspoon pure vanilla extract

¼ teaspoon ground nutmeg

1 tablespoon vegetable oil

About ⅓ cup ice cream crumbles* or other sprinkles

I like to use ice cream crumbles (like Dean Jacobs) for their soft cookie crumb texture. Plus, they come in flavors like orange cream.

1 In a large food processor, process cookies to fine crumbs. With the machine off, add brown sugar, cinnamon, nutmeg, and vanilla; cover and process until blended. Continue to process while adding oil through the feed tube.

2 Add just enough water to achieve the consistency of creamy peanut butter, about ⅓ to ½ cup. In a clean jar, layer and/or top with ice cream crumbles or other sprinkles. Store in the refrigerator in an airtight container for up to 1 month.

TAKE IT A STEP FURTHER

Cookie Butter Frosting: Slather this sweet, creamy cookie-flavored spread onto cakes and cookies or sandwich it between graham crackers for an after-school snack. With an electric mixer on medium-high speed, beat to combine ½ cup room temperature unsalted butter and ½ cup cookie butter. Beat for 2 to 3 minutes, or until smooth. Add 1 teaspoon pure vanilla extract. Slowly beat in 1 cup confectioners' sugar, followed by 1 tablespoon milk and then another 1 cup confectioners' sugar. If you want a creamier frosting, add another 1 to 2 tablespoons milk and beat until smooth.

Layer sprinkles—any kind you like—into Cookie Butter Frosting immediately before spreading it onto your confections. Don't bother mixing them into straight Cookie Butter—they'll just disappear. Instead, decorate with loads of sprinkles on top right before serving.

an easy do-it-yourself version of a classic

❖ Homemade Pop Tarts ❖

MAKES 10 TO 12 MINI TARTS

The fronts of these twee tarts are tiny blank canvases. Try decorating them in a way that hints at what's inside, using with the same colors and flavors as the filling. If you'd like, make the tarts more healthful by filling them with low-sugar fruit preserves.

1 roll of store-bought pie dough, cold

Assorted fruit preserves

1 egg, beaten

About 1½ cups Royal Icing (page 46)

⅓ cup assorted sprinkles*

*Here's what I used (left). Row 1: blue licorice candies with robin's-egg blue pearlized dragées; multicolored butterfly confetti; Sno-Caps; spring mix confetti shaped like bunnies. Row 2: crushed yellow hard candy with yellow sanding sugar; green jumbo quins with white marshmallow bits; purple nonpareils with multicolored jimmies; yellow Jordan almonds with yellow and white star confetti. Row 3: orange gourmet jelly beans; pink pearlized dragées with red, pink, and white nonpareils; blue diamond confetti with blue quins and white snowflakes; white pearlized jimmies with a peppermint candy and red Sixlet.

1 Preheat oven to 375°F. Line a baking sheet with parchment paper or a silicone baking mat.

2 Cut cold dough into two equal pieces and roll it into rectangles about 6 by 10 inches and ¼ inch thick. Spread tablespoonfuls of filling in rows spaced about ½ inch apart, leaving a ½-inch border around the edges of the dough.

3 Using a pastry brush, paint egg wash around and between the filling. Gently place the second piece of dough on top and press around the filling to seal. Use a sharp knife or pizza cutter to cut dough into 2-by-4-inch rectangles and press the edges of each tart with the tines of a fork to seal. Arrange tarts on prepared baking sheet and brush tops with a bit more egg wash.

4 Bake for 10 to 12 minutes, or until golden brown around the edges. Let cool.

5 Spread icing onto cooled pastries using an offset spatula. Decorate with sprinkles.

MIX-AND-MATCH FLAVORS AND FROSTINGS

Ideas for fillings include chocolate hazelnut spread, marshmallow fluff, jams, jellies, preserves, marmalade, Sprinkles Pastry Cream (page 95), store-bought or homemade cookie butter (page 42), or any other spreadable goodness you can dream up.

If fruit preserves and other fillings are difficult to spread, microwave them for a few seconds and stir until smooth.

baking recipe royalty

Royal Icing

MAKES ABOUT 2½ CUPS

Perfect for finishing everything from cookies and cakes to homemade
pop tarts (page 45), royal icing is an indispensable decorating tool.
Divide it among bowls and tint it a rainbow of colors.

2 egg whites*
1 tablespoon lemon juice
3 cups confectioners' sugar
A few drops food coloring,
optional

*I like to use 2 teaspoons
pasteurized egg white, such as
Just Egg Whites.

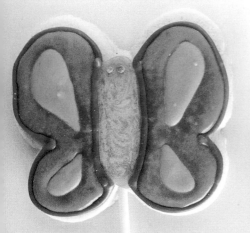

1 Using an electric mixer fitted with the whisk attachment, whisk together all ingredients for several minutes on high speed until the mixture is thick, shiny, and opaque white. It should have the consistency of glue. If it is too thin, add more powdered sugar, a teaspoonful at a time, as needed. If it is too thick, add water, a teaspoonful at a time, as needed.

2 Divide icing among bowls and add food coloring to achieve desired hues. While you work, keep the bowls covered to keep the icing from drying out and hardening.

DECORATING WITH ROYAL ICING

Springtime Cookie Pops: Use your favorite cookie cutters to cut out shapes from rolled sugar-cookie dough. Insert sticks into the base of the cookie, being sure not to let the stick poke out the back of the cookie. To decorate, draw outlines with royal icing onto the cookies using a pastry bag fitted with a thin tip (#2) and let dry. Then flood the outlines with more royal icing. The icing will stay inside the lines you've drawn.

Thin and smooth, this classic topping dries to a shiny, hard surface that has a soft crunch when you bite into it. Pastry chefs love it for its adaptability and the polish it adds to baked goods. You can spread it on with a spatula or load it into a pastry bag fitted with a metal tip. (If you don't have a pastry bag, you can DIY one with a ziptop plastic bag. Load icing into it, twist the bag just above the icing, and snip off ¼ inch of one of the bottom corners to pipe out icing.)

Breakfast Sweets

46

chunky, chewy, chocolate-malty

Malted Milk Ball Crispy Treats

MAKES 12 3-INCH TREATS

Glimmering rows of malt balls accented in gold add an elegance to these crispy treats that elevates them above the bake sale.

4 cups malted milk balls, divided

1 (10-ounce) package large marshmallows

¼ cup (½ stick) unsalted butter

1 tablespoon unsweetened cocoa powder

3 cups crisp rice cereal, such as Rice Krispies

1 cup chocolate-flavored puffed cereal, such as Cocoa Puffs

¾ cup malted milk powder*

½ cup dark chocolate melts or chocolate chips

Spray-on gold glitter

1 tablespoon gold sugar or gold sanding sugar

Malted milk powder is a sweetener made from barley malt. It's the key ingredient in old-fashioned milkshakes, malt balls, and these tasty crispy treats.

1 Coat a 9-by-12-inch pan with cooking spray. Chop 1 cup of the malted milk balls in half.

2 In a large saucepan, combine marshmallows, butter, and cocoa powder. Cook and stir over medium-low heat until melted, about 3-5 minutes. Remove from heat; stir in cereals, malted milk powder, and chopped malted milk balls. Press mixture into prepared pan. Let sit at room temperature for 5-10 minutes, or until cool and firm.

3 Microwave chocolate melts or chips for 1 minute on full power. Stir until smooth. Pour into pan and spread in a thin layer over cereal mixture. Quickly, before the chocolate hardens, top with even rows of malted milk balls.

4 Spray the top of the treats lightly with edible gold spray and dust with gold sugar while the spray is still wet. Cut into 3-inch squares and serve.

It's not easy to chop malted milk balls—they roll! Carefully cut them in half with a large, sharp knife. Then lay them on their flat side before continuing.

glittery, glamorous brunch cocktails

·❖· Sparkling Stone Fruit White Sangria ·❖·

MAKES 4 TO 6 GLASSES

Stone fruits—nectarines, peaches, mangoes, plums, and apricots—are bursting with flavors of summer. A pitcher of this sparkling white wine and fruit concoction is a refreshing addition at brunch, on picnics, or anytime you want a little extra sunshine.

SANGRIA

1 nectarine

1 plum

1 peach

1 apricot

½ cup fresh blackberries or raspberries

1 (750 milliliter) bottle white wine*

¼ cup orange liqueur (such as Cointreau or Mandarine Napoleon)

ICE

2 cups sparkling water

¼ cup edible gold metallic glitter

*Try a crisp, fruity Spanish white wine such as albariño.

1 To cut the stone fruits, run a sharp knife around the edge of each fruit. Twist to separate the halves; discard pit. Cut halves into ½-inch wedges.

2 Combine fruit, wine, and liqueur in a large pitcher and chill for at least 1 hour to let the flavors meld. To serve, add ice and sparkling water before stirring in glitter.

PLAN AHEAD

You can combine the wine, liqueur, and fruits a few days in advance—the flavors will improve the longer the sangria sits. Just add sparkling water, ice, and glitter right before serving so it doesn't dissolve.

Add a pinch of edible glitter to any cocktail! Or try glitter in cocktail glass rims, as on page 50.

Mix-and-Match Cocktail Rims

There are endless ways to rim glasses with sprinkles. Light types such as sanding sugar will stick with thin substances, like lemon juice or even water, while quins and pearls require a liquid with more substance, like coconut milk or sweetened condensed milk, to help them adhere. For really heavy sprinkles, such as quins and sixlets, rim the glass with melted chocolate or candy melts, which will dry hard and firmly hold the sprinkles in place.

POSSIBLE MOISTENERS

milk

spirits

melted chocolate

candy coating in all different colors

citrus and other fruit juices

POSSIBLE SPRINKLES

crushed candies

crushed cookies (like Oreos)

jimmies

nonpareils

tinted and/or flavored sanding sugars

flaked or shredded coconut

crushed candied bacon

fancy salts

edible glitter

Try mixing and matching sprinkles and a variety of moisteners. Experiment with a mix of sprinkles or all one kind. Pour a moistener into a shallow dish that's wider than your cocktail glasses. Put sprinkles in a separate dish (or multiple dishes, for a layered look). Hold each glass by the stem and swirl the rim in moistener, then dunk it in sprinkles. Let dry before adding beverages to sprinkles-rimmed glasses.

swizzle sticks made of rock sugar

Rock Candy Garnishes

MAKES 4

Instead of—or in addition to—jazzing up your cocktail glass with sprinkle-bedazzled rims, now you can dress up your drinks with these crystalized gems. Sanding sugar, edible glitter, tinted and flavored sugars, and small nonpareils work best for adding glitter to rock candy because they're small and light and won't fall off.

4 rock candy sticks, store-bought or homemade (page 135)

About ¼ cup sanding sugar, glitter, mini nonpareils, or a mix

Quickly dunk store-bought or homemade rock candy sticks (for recipe, see page 135) in a glass of water or juice. Next, dip them in sprinkles or sparkling sugars to coat. For a multilayered look, dip sticks in several different types of sprinkles. Let dry. Serve alongside cocktails or propped across glasses; your guests can enjoy the candy sticks separately or use them as drink stirrers. (Note: If you insert the sticks in the cocktails before serving, the sprinkles may dissolve into the drinks too soon.)

Rock candy garnishes are particularly lovely with champagne and sparkling wines. Sparkling cider or lemonade would make for a fun kids' party punch.

triple-chocolate crispy cookies originally from Italy

⊶ Chocolate Pistachio Biscotti ⊷

MAKES 2 DOZEN

Biscotti means "twice baked" in Italian. First you form the crumbly dough into one stiff mass and bake it whole. Then you let it cool, slice it, and bake it again at a lower temperature. That's what gives biscotti an almost crackerlike quality, which goes especially well with coffee. This triple-chocolate double-baked treat is dipped in a dark chocolate coating with sprinkles on top. Dip it in your coffee and then pop it in your mouth.

2 cups all-purpose flour

¾ cup unsweetened cocoa powder

½ teaspoon baking soda

⅛ teaspoon salt

3 large eggs

1 cup packed light brown sugar

4 tablespoons unsalted butter, softened

1 tablespoon pure vanilla extract

1 teaspoon pure almond extract

1 teaspoon ground coffee

½ cup bittersweet chocolate chips

1 cup shelled pistachios

About ½ cup (4 ounces) colored candy melts*

About ⅓ cup red nonpareils, or any other sprinkles

See page 79 for more on how to melt and dip candy melts.

1 Preheat oven to 350°F. Line 2 baking sheets with parchment paper or silicone baking mats. In a large bowl, whisk flour, cocoa powder, baking soda, and salt. Using an electric mixer on low speed, beat in eggs for about 1 minute, until a crumbly dough forms.

2 In a separate large bowl, beat brown sugar with butter, extracts, and coffee until combined. Add sugar mixture to flour mixture and beat on low speed until a dough begins to form. It will not come together completely. Fold in chocolate chips and pistachios.

3 Turn out dough onto a lightly floured surface. Press dough together with your hands, forming it into one mass. Then divide it into two equal parts and form it into two logs. Place one log on each prepared baking sheet and press it with the palm of your hand to flatten to a width of about 3 inches.

4 Bake for 20 minutes, rotating the pans halfway through the baking time. Remove from oven and lower oven temperature to 250°F. Let dough rest on pans for 20 minutes. Dough will be slightly spongy to the touch, similar to a dense bread.

5 Transfer logs to a cutting board. Using a serrated knife, cut into ½-inch slices. Return the slices, cut side up, to the baking sheets. Bake for another 40 minutes. Transfer cookies to wire racks to cool.

6 Melt candy melts in a deep mug or bowl according to package directions. Dip cooled biscotti halfway in melted candy melts. Place on parchment paper and decorate with dragées and sprinkles.

chocolate-covered marshmallows

·❖· Hot Chocolate Stir Sticks ·❖·

MAKES 10

M'mmm, hot chocolate. Sure, it's delicious, but where's the pizzazz? Here!
These chocolate-covered-marshmallow stirring sticks, topped with crushed peppermint
candy and sprinkles, add both color and flavor to every cozy cup.

8 ounces chocolate*

10 marshmallows

10 cocktail picks, candy sticks, or bamboo skewers

About 1 cup crushed peppermint candies or candy canes

2 tablespoons sprinkles**

*Bittersweet, semisweet, milk, white, or dark chocolate— all are delicious in this recipe. Choose your favorite.

**I like to use red sparkling sugar, white nonpareils, pearlized jimmies, or a mix of all three.

1 Line a baking sheet or large tray with parchment paper.

2 Melt chocolate in the microwave or a glass or metal bowl set over a pot of simmering water, stirring frequently.

3 Skewer each marshmallow on a stick. Dip marshmallows in chocolate and then in crushed peppermint candies and sprinkles. Place on the lined baking sheet to cool. Allow to set for at least 15 minutes before serving.

MORE TO TRY

Double-Dipped Stir Sticks: For an extra-decadent treat, melt two kinds of chocolate. Let the first chocolate layer dry before dipping into the second, and let a bit of the first layer show for a beautiful layered look.

Mini Stir Sticks: Swap 20 to 30 mini marshmallows for the 10 regular ones and skewer with toothpicks.

S'Mores Stir Sticks: Dip chocolate-dunked marshmallows in crushed graham crackers instead of peppermint candies. Decorate with chocolate jimmies or white nonpareils.

Cookies, Cakes, and Pies

Whether it's a handful of hearts on the edge of Red Velvet Whoopie Pies, a dainty and delicate decoration on Embroidered Sugar Cookies, or the bright bursts of color in a fresh take on the classic Confetti Layer Cake, every sweet treat is better with a little sparkle. Fleck cute Holiday Cake Pops with festive bits-n-pieces, or tuck sprinkles in unexpected places with Key Lime Pie and Sprinkles Pastry Cream for a touch of whimsy you'll really bake a shine to.

a twist on the iconic New York City treat

Black and White Cookies

MAKES 10 TO 12 COOKIES

These soft and cakey half-and-half cookies are the perfect
palette for your favorite sprinkles, jimmies, confetti, or dragées
in elegant shades of black and white.

COOKIES

4 cups cake flour, sifted

½ teaspoon baking powder

½ teaspoon salt

1 cup unsalted butter, at room
temperature

1¾ cups sugar

½ teaspoon pure vanilla extract

½ teaspoon lemon extract*

4 egg whites

¾ cups milk

ICING

6 cups confectioners' sugar

½ cup plus 1 tablespoon milk

1½ teaspoons pure vanilla extract

4 tablespoons cocoa powder

About 4 tablespoons each
chocolate jimmies, white jimmies
and white Sixlets, or other
sprinkles**

*The lightly lemony flavor is
a trademark of these soft
vanilla cookies. If desired, you
can omit the lemon extract and
achieve a pure vanilla flavor.*

**Any type will work well.
Try metallic or pearlized sprinkles
for a dazzling effect.*

1 Preheat oven to 375°F. Line two baking sheets with parchment paper or silicone baking mats. Sift flour, baking powder, and salt into a medium bowl.

2 In a stand mixer, beat butter on medium to medium-high speed for several minutes, until smooth. Reduce speed to low and add sugar in a slow stream. Beat butter and sugar on medium-high speed for several minutes until light and fluffy. Beat in vanilla extract, then lemon extract, and then egg whites, mixing to combine after each addition. Add flour mixture and milk in three alternating additions and mix until just combined.

3 Drop ¼-cup scoops of dough about 5 inches apart onto cookie sheets. Moisten a small offset spatula or butter knife with water and spread each mound of dough into a flat 3-inch round. Bake for 8 to 10 minutes, rotating sheets halfway through baking, just until cookie edges start to turn golden.

4 For the icing, mix confectioners' sugar, milk, and vanilla in a bowl until smooth. Transfer half of the icing to another bowl and add cocoa powder. Mix until no cocoa powder lumps remain.

5 Using a small offset spatula, spread the chocolate icing on half the cookie. Repeat with the vanilla icing on the other half. Return iced cookies to wire racks to set for 30 minutes and then remove them with a spatula. Store cookies in an airtight container, layered between wax paper, for up to 3 days.

For a nontraditional look, frost these cookies in either all white or all chocolate icing. Decorate with matching or contrasting sprinkles.

sparkling stained-glass confections

❖ Windowpane Cookies ❖

MAKES ABOUT 45 COOKIES

Thanks to colorful translucent candies, these cookies look like gorgeously intricate cut-glass windowpanes. Use candies in festive hues and two sizes of cookie cutters to create these special treats. Think red hearts for Valentine's Day, pastel flowers for spring, and emerald evergreens for the winter holidays.

1 batch Sugar Cookie Dough (page 63)

About ½ cup various sanding sugars,* sorted by color

Clear hard candies like Jolly Ranchers can be used instead. Just sort them by color into ziptop plastic bags, seal, and use a hammer to crush the candies into bits.

1 Preheat oven to 350°F. Line several baking sheets with silicone baking mats or parchment paper.

2 On a lightly floured work surface, roll dough to a thickness of ¼ inch. Cut out shapes using the larger cookie cutter and then use the smaller cutters to remove "windows" from those shapes. Arrange cookies about 1 inch apart on prepared baking sheets.

3 Place candies in plastic zip-top bags (one color per bag), seal bags, and crush them with a rolling pin or meat mallet. Fill cookie windows with crushed candy pieces.

4 Bake for 8 to 10 minutes, or until edges start to turn golden, rotating sheets halfway through baking time. Place sheets on wire racks to cool for a few minutes before gently removing cookies with a metal spatula. Let cookies cool completely on wire racks. Store between layers of wax paper to prevent sticking in an airtight container for up to 1 week.

EDIBLE ORNAMENTS

It's fun to make Windowpane Cookies (and other festive rolled cookies, like the Gingerbreads on page 86) into holiday ornaments. Use a bamboo skewer or chopstick to poke a hole about ¾ inch from the top of each cookie before baking. Once baked cookies have cooled, thread 10 inches of ribbon or colorful bakers' twine through each hole and tie in a bow.

❖ Embroidered Sugar Cookies ❖

MAKES ABOUT 2 DOZEN COOKIES

Now's your chance to take your "embroidery" and baking skills to the next level with this twist on a sugar cookie classic. Honestly, what better compliment could a stitching artist receive than to have her work devoured by a hungry public?

SUGAR COOKIE DOUGH

1⅔ cups all-purpose flour

½ teaspoon baking powder

¼ teaspoon salt

½ cup (1 stick) unsalted butter, softened

¾ cup plus 2 tablespoons sugar

1 egg, at room temperature, beaten

1 teaspoon pure vanilla extract

FROSTING AND TOPPING

3 cups Royal Icing (page 46), or Sugar Cookie Frosting (page 64)

⅓ cup tinted sanding sugar

½ cup amount jimmies, in several colors

¼ cup yellow dragées

1 Sift together flour, baking powder, and salt into a bowl.

2 In another bowl cream butter and sugar with an electric mixer on medium speed for 2 to 3 minutes, or until light and fluffy. Beat in egg and vanilla. Mix in flour mixture until dough is smooth and firm.

3 Divide dough in half and shape into two ½-inch-thick disks. Cover them in plastic wrap and refrigerate for 2 hours. (At this point the dough can be covered in plastic wrap, sealed in a zip-top plastic bag, and frozen for up to 2 weeks.)

4 Preheat oven to 325°F. Line several baking sheets with parchment paper.

5 Place dough on a lightly floured surface and dust dough with more flour. Gently roll each disk to a thickness of ⅛ inch. Using a cookie cutter, cut out cookies and then place about 1 inch apart on prepared sheets.

6 Bake for 10 to 15 minutes, rotating sheets halfway through baking, until edges are golden brown. Transfer cookies to wire racks with a metal spatula and let cool.

7 Decorate cookies with icing, colored sugars, and sprinkles. Use clean hands or kitchen tweezers to place jimmies on cookies in a decorative pattern. For flowers, place 1 dragée at the center of each blossom.

Draw inspiration for cookie decoration from embroidery, cross-stitch, or your favorite floral patterns.

smooth, creamy, decadent

Sugar Cookie Frosting

MAKES 3 CUPS

This delicious cream-cheese-based frosting stays soft long enough for you to decorate your cookies, and then it develops a smooth, slightly shiny surface that holds the sprinkles in place. It's a softer alternative to royal icing.

1 (8-ounce) package cream cheese

1 cup confectioners' sugar, sifted, plus more to taste

2 tablespoons milk

1 teaspoon pure vanilla extract

¼ to ½ cup sprinkles, if desired

1 In the bowl of a stand mixer on medium speed, beat cream cheese for 1 minute, or until creamy and soft. Add confectioners' sugar, milk, and vanilla and beat for 1 minute, or until smooth and fluffy.

2 Increase mixer speed to medium-high and beat for 3 minutes more, or until no lumps remain. Taste and beat in sprinkles (if necessary) and more confectioners' sugar as needed.

Buttercream Frosting

MAKES 2 CUPS

Everyone needs a good buttercream frosting recipe.
Here's yours.

1 cup (2 sticks) unsalted butter,
at room temperature
3 cups confectioners' sugar, sifted
1 to 2 tablespoons heavy cream
1 tablespoon pure vanilla extract
About ⅓ cup sprinkles, optional

1 With an electric mixer on medium-high speed, beat butter for 1 minute, or until creamy and soft. Add confectioners' sugar, ½ cup at a time, beating to incorporate after each addition. Gradually beat in heavy cream until smooth.

2 Scrape down the sides of the bowl with a rubber spatula. Add vanilla—and sprinkles, if using—and beat for 1 minute more, or until soft and fluffy. Use immediately or refrigerate, covered, for up to 5 days.

You can swirl sprinkles into buttercream before frosting your treats, or frost first and then arrange the sprinkles on top.

Chocolate Buttercream Frosting
After incorporating the confectioners' sugar, add 8 ounces melted and cooled semisweet chocolate (or bittersweet or dark chocolate, if you prefer) to the mixture and beat until soft and fluffy. Then add cream.

the cream filling is a sweet surprise

⊹ Strawberry Teacup Cupcakes ⊹

MAKES 24 CUPCAKES

Baked in oven-safe teacups, these darling cupcakes are ideal for
tea parties, birthday parties, and baby showers. Fill them with strawberry
preserves or Sprinkles Pastry Cream—or both!—for a hidden treat.

CAKE

3 cups cake flour, sifted

1¼ teaspoons baking powder

1 teaspoon salt

1 cup (2 sticks) unsalted butter,
room temperature

2¼ cups sugar

1 teaspoon pure vanilla extract

4 egg whites, divided

1 cup milk*

FILLING, FROSTING,
AND TOPPING

About ½ cup strawberry fruit
spread or preserves, if desired

About ½ cup Sprinkles Pastry
Cream (page 95), if desired

3 cups Buttercream Frosting
(page 65)

¼ to ½ cup assorted sprinkles

*For extra flavor, use strawberry-
flavored milk or coconut milk.*

1 Preheat oven to 350°F. Grease 18 oven-safe teacups with cooking spray or butter, or line them with cupcake liners.

2 In a medium bowl, whisk to combine flour, baking powder, and salt.

3 In another bowl, beat butter and sugar with an electric mixer on medium-high speed until light and fluffy, about 5 minutes. Scrape down the sides of the bowl. Add vanilla and beat for 1 minute more. Beat in egg whites, one at a time, scraping down the sides of the bowl after each addition. Beat in flour mixture and milk in three alternating additions, starting and ending with flour mixture. Scoop batter into prepared teacups until each is about three-quarters full and place on a rimmed baking sheet.

4 Bake for about 20 minutes, until a toothpick inserted in the center of a cupcake comes out clean. Let cool.

5 With a paring knife, cut a 1-inch cone shape out of the center of each cooled cupcake. Pinch off and discard the tip of each cone. Fill cupcakes with strawberry preserves and/or Sprinkles Pastry Cream and replace tops. Generously spread or pipe on buttercream frosting, checking to make sure the seam on top of each cupcake are covered. Top with assorted sprinkles.

Use only teacups you're sure are oven-safe. To find out if yours are, flip it over! Most will say so on the bottom.

PLAN AHEAD

*Sealed in an airtight container, this batter will keep for
1 month.*

Stenciling with Sprinkles

Take your sprinkle art to the next level! Gorgeous patterns and intricate designs are easy to create with doilies, cookie cutters, paper cutouts, lace, and other creative stencils.

POSSIBLE TOPPINGS
Buttercream Frosting (page 65)
Chocolate Buttercream Frosting (page 65)
Royal Icing (page 46)
Sugar Cookie Frosting (page 64)

POSSIBLE SPRINKLES
confectioners' sugar
sanding sugar
small nonpareils
cocoa powder

First, bake and frost any confection you like. Before the frosting sets, gently place one or multiple stencils on top. Shake sprinkles inside (or outside) the shapes of the pattern and then carefully remove the stencil. Use number cookie cutters for birthdays, letter cookie cutters for personalized gifts, and seasonal shapes for holiday-themed parties (for more ideas, see page 23).

You can work inside or outside cookie cutters for a stunning effect. If you have trouble keeping sprinkles where you want them, trace your stencil onto parchment paper or wax paper, cut out the solid shape, and place that on the frosting. Then add your sprinkles and remove the shape when you're done.

party perfect

⋯⟡ Confetti Layer Cake ⟡⋯

MAKES 1 TRIPLE LAYER CAKE

When sprinkles (aka jimmies) are folded into cake batter,
they typically melt away during baking, leaving behind little confetti-like
poufs of color. In this deconstructed version of the birthday cake,
the crusts are removed to show off the sprinkles hidden inside.

CAKE

1½ cups milk

9 large egg whites, lightly beaten

⅓ cup applesauce

1 tablespoon pure vanilla extract

½ teaspoon almond extract

4½ cups cake flour, sifted, plus
more for flouring pans

2 tablespoons baking powder

1½ teaspoons salt

1 cup (2 sticks) unsalted butter,
at room temperature

2 cups sugar

½ cup rainbow jimmies

FROSTING AND TOPPING

4 cups Buttercream Frosting
(page 65)

¼ cup rainbow jimmies*

*If you want sprinkles to retain
their shape when baked into
cakes, go for Wilton's
ColorBurst Batter Bits.*

1 Preheat oven to 350°F. Coat three 9-inch round cake pans with cooking spray and dust with flour.

2 In a medium bowl, stir milk, egg whites, applesauce, and extracts. Into another bowl, sift together flour, baking powder, and salt.

3 Beat butter and sugar with an electric mixer on medium speed until light and fluffy, about 5 minutes. Reduce mixer speed to low and add flour and milk mixtures in three alternating additions, starting and ending with flour mixture. Fold in rainbow sprinkles.

4 Divide batter evenly among pans. Bake until a cake tester inserted in the centers comes out clean, 25 to 30 minutes.

5 Cool cakes in pans set on wire racks for 5 minutes. Run a knife around the sides of each pan and invert cakes onto a cutting board. With a serrated knife, carefully cut off the tops and "crusts," exposing the confetti sprinkles baked inside.

6 Place one cake layer on a cake stand. Spread ¾ cup buttercream evenly over top. Top with a second cake layer, spread with another ¾ cup buttercream, and top with the third cake layer. Spread remaining buttercream evenly over top, leaving the sides exposed. Decorate the perimeter of the top with rainbow jimmies. Serve or store, refrigerated, for up to 3 days.

For a pretty finish, fit a piping bag with a round metal tip and fill with buttercream. Pipe a neat ring of frosting around each layer and pipe the top of the cake with concentric circles, if desired.

How to Cover a Cake with Sprinkles

Cakes, cupcakes, cookies, brownies, and other baked goods look fantastic when completely adorned in sprinkles. Your kitchen, on the other hand, does not. Here's a way to achieve this effect without making a major mess.

1 Frost a cake in buttercream, smooth the edges for a flat frosted surface, and freeze it until the frosting feels hard, about 15 minutes.

2 Place the cake on a cardboard circle on a jellyroll pan (a baking sheet with a lip), making sure the pan is longer than the edge of the cake. Pour about ½ cup sprinkles on top (nonpareils work best).

3 Gently press to cover the top of the cake in sprinkles, adding more as necessary.

4 Press a handful of sprinkles into the side of the cake, as shown. Repeat until the cake is covered.

5 Spoon additional sprinkles on top of the cake and smooth them onto the edges with a spatula, pressing gently to make sure they adhere to the buttercream. Using your hands, carefully press more sprinkles into any bare areas along the side of the cake, and then smooth them down with your spatula. Voilà!

Cookies, Cakes, and Pies

a party-perfect celebration

❖ Rainbow Layer Cake ❖

MAKES 1 SIX-LAYER CAKE

This bright, multihued cake is a festive addition to any party. For a full-color effect, dye the layers to match a rainbow. Or let your imagination take flight. Create your own palette by tinting the cake layers to coordinate with the jimmies, nonpareils, or dragées of your choice.

6 egg whites (about ⅔ cup), at room temperature

1 cup sugar, divided

1 cup (2 sticks) unsalted butter, at room temperature

3 tablespoons applesauce

2 teaspoons pure vanilla extract

2 whole eggs

2¼ cups cake flour

2 teaspoons baking powder

Pinch salt

6 different hues of food coloring

2 cups Buttercream Frosting (page 65)*

2 cups rainbow sprinkles, nonpareils, and/or pearl dragées

Jams, jellies, and other fillings also work well.

1 Preheat oven to 350°F. Line six 6-inch cake pans with parchment paper.

2 Beat egg whites with an electric mixer on medium-high speed until foamy, about 2 minutes. Increase mixer speed to high and continue beating until soft peaks form, about 3 minutes. Gradually add ½ cup of the sugar, continuing to beat until stiff peaks form, about 3 minutes more.

3 In another large mixing bowl, cream butter and the remaining ½ cup of sugar on medium speed until light and fluffy and increased in volume, about 5 minutes. Add applesauce, vanilla, and eggs and mix on medium speed for 1 minute more.

4 Sift together flour, baking powder, and salt. Add to butter mixture and mix on medium speed for 1 minute. Pour in ¾ cup water and mix to combine. Fold in egg whites with a large spatula.

5 Divide batter evenly among 6 small bowls. Starting with the lightest color, tint batter with food coloring, whisking in a few drops at a time until the desired intensity is reached. Pour each of the colored batters into a different parchment-lined cake pan (each should be half full) and bake until a toothpick inserted in the center comes out clean, about 12 to 15 minutes.

6 Stack layers according to the colors of the rainbow, spreading a thin layer buttercream between each. Using an offset spatula, frost the whole cake with a thin layer of buttercream.

7 Place cake on a freezer-safe plate. Freeze for 15 minutes, or until buttercream is firm. Remove from freezer and cover cake in sprinkles, following the tutorial on page 72.

Cookies, Cakes, and Pies

for your sweetheart

❖ Red Velvet Whoopie Pies ❖

MAKES 2 DOZEN

The first time I saw the deep crimson hue of a red velvet cake I was captivated. Show your true love how much you care by presenting them with not just one, but a whole stack of Red Velvet Whoopie Pies edged with extra big heart-shaped confetti.

CAKE

2 cups all-purpose flour

3 tablespoons unsweetened cocoa powder

½ teaspoon baking soda

½ teaspoon salt

4 tablespoons (½ stick) unsalted butter, softened

¼ cup vegetable oil

1 cup sugar

1 large egg

1 teaspoon pure vanilla extract

1 teaspoon distilled white vinegar

⅔ cup buttermilk

Several drops red food coloring*

⅓ cup large red heart-shaped confetti

⅓ cup small red, pink, and white heart-shaped confetti

FILLING

1 (8-ounce) package cream cheese

¼ teaspoon salt

1 cup powdered sugar

1 tablespoon pure vanilla extract

1½ cups heavy cream

*India Tree makes an all-natural red food coloring derived from beets.

1 Preheat oven to 350°F. Line two baking sheets with parchment paper or silicone baking mats.

2 Whisk together flour, cocoa powder, baking soda, and salt in a large bowl.

3 In a second large bowl, beat butter, oil, and sugar with an electric mixer on medium speed until thoroughly combined, about 2 minutes. Beat in egg, vanilla, and vinegar. Reduce mixer speed to low and mix in flour mixture and buttermilk in three alternating additions. With mixer still on low speed, beat in food coloring 1 or 2 drops at a time to produce the desired shade.

4 Spoon 2-tablespoon mounds of batter 2 inches apart on lined baking sheets. Bake until rounds are puffed and set, 8 to 10 minutes. Slide parchment with rounds onto wire racks to cool completely.

5 Beat cream cheese, salt, sugar, and vanilla with an electric mixer on medium speed until fluffy, about 1 minute. With the mixer still running, drizzle in heavy cream. Continue beating for about 5 minutes more, until stiff peaks form. Refrigerate until ready to use, up to 3 days.

6 Spread about ¼ cup filling on the flat side of half of the rounds and top with the unfrosted rounds. Place sprinkles in a shallow bowl. Roll the edges of the pies in the sprinkles to coat.

Sweet and Spicy! If you want your red velvet whoopie pies to taste more like they look, add a dose of cinnamon (¼ teaspoon), and if you are really brave, a touch of ground cayenne pepper (about ⅛ teaspoon will do).

Cookies, Cakes, and Pies

chocolate in liquid form

Melted Chocolate

MAKES 2 CUPS MELTED CHOCOLATE

Chocolate chips, chunks, candy melts, or your favorite chocolate bar are all good candidates for melting. High-quality chocolate is fairly delicate and is best melted over low heat using the double-boiler method. For everyday chocolate melting, a microwave works just fine.

Roughly chop at least 1 pound chocolate (about 2 cups) into ½- to 1-inch pieces. Melt using one of the following methods. Note that tempering is just the double-boiler method, with the help of a candy thermometer and a little extra patience.

Water is the enemy of melted chocolate. Just one droplet can make melting chocolate seize up and become chunky and unusable.

Microwave Method: Place chocolate pieces in a heatproof bowl. Heat in microwave for 60 seconds, stirring halfway through. Stir until any remaining lumps dissolve. Chocolate burns easily, so avoid overcooking.

Double-Boiler Method: Place chocolate pieces in the top of a double boiler or a heatproof bowl that fits snugly inside the top of a saucepan of water. To prevent burning, make sure the water doesn't touch the bottom of the bowl. Bring to a simmer over low heat. Stir chocolate occasionally with a rubber spatula until melted, about 5 minutes.

Tempering Method: Tempering is not always necessary, but it is the key to a shiny, smooth-looking chocolate coating. You will need a candy thermometer. Melt about two-thirds of the chopped chocolate in the top of a double boiler or a heatproof bowl that fits snugly inside the top of a saucepan of water. To prevent burning, make sure water doesn't touch the bottom of the bowl. Bring to a simmer over medium-low heat until temperature reaches 115°F, stirring constantly. Remove from heat and stir in the rest of the chocolate, which will help reduce the temperature. Continue to stir. Once the temperature reaches 85°F, remove any chunks; stir and reheat until the temperature reaches 90°F, perfect for dipping.

dip, dunk, coat!

Candy Melts

MAKES 1 CUP MELTED CANDY

Candy melts are small disks of candy that come in different colors and flavors, including white and dark chocolate. They melt in the microwave lickety-split and make dipping and coating sprinkles treats oh so easy. Pretzels, strawberries, marshmallows, cookies, cake pops, vanilla wafers—whatever you dunk and decorate will instantly become ten times more delicious than it was before!

1 cup candy melts
1 teaspoon shortening, optional

Put the melts in a medium heatproof bowl. Microwave for 60 seconds, stirring halfway though. Stir the melted candy with a butter knife until smooth. If too thick for dipping, stir in shortening.

Tip: Stir candy melts with a butter knife; they tend to get stuck inside the hollow of a spoon.

lovely lollies

⟫ Holiday Cake Pops ⟪

MAKES 1 DOZEN

Add a little more sparkle to your holidays
with these silver and gold cake pops.

1 (18¼-ounce) box cake mix,
any flavor

About three-fourths of 1
(16-ounce) container prepared
frosting, any flavor*

1 pound (16 ounces) white
chocolate candy melts, preferably
Belcolate White Chocolate**

1 to 2 teaspoons vegetable oil

12 lollipop sticks

Large foam block, optional,
for drying***

½ cup metallic sprinkles,
nonpareils, and colored sugars
of your choice

⅛ to ¼ teaspoon metallic luster
dust and/or spray-on glitter,
such as Color Mist

*Dark-colored cakes may
require a second coating
of white chocolate.*

**Real white chocolate such
as Belcolate has a smooth
cream-colored finish.*

*** To create completely round
cake pops, dry them upright by
pushing the sticks into a large
foam block. Alternatively, you
can place them upside down
onto the lined baking sheet,
sticks pointing up.*

1 Line a large baking sheet with parchment or wax paper.

2 Prepare cake according to the package directions in any size pan. Let cool. Crumble the cooled cake into a large bowl. Mix frosting into cake crumbs ½ cup at a time until the mixture has the consistency of a firm dough. Roll it into 1½-inch balls. Place balls on the lined baking sheet and freeze for at least 15 minutes. (Frozen cake balls won't fall apart during dipping, and the chocolate sets faster.)

3 Melt white chocolate in a heatproof bowl, either over a pan of simmering water or with 30-second bursts of high power in the microwave, stirring after each interval until smooth. Dip about 1 inch of each lollipop stick into melted chocolate and immediately insert into cake balls. Return to the lined baking sheet.

4 Dip pops into the candy coating and spin to cover completely. Decorate with pearlescent or metallic dragées, nonpareils, or whatever sprinkles you like. Let dry before painting on luster dust with a brush dipped in vodka or applying spray-on glitter.

FUN WITH METALLICS

Explore different metallic sprinkles, dusts, and coatings. The pops can be coated with gold or silver edible spray paint. Or, for an extra layer of shimmer, shake on edible glitter or sanding sugar while the spray is still wet.

two confections rolled into one

❖ Banana Split Trifle Cake ❖

SERVES 6 TO 8

A banana split is a delicious mishmash of flavors and toppings, all coexisting in the same dish. Here I've married this ice cream parlor favorite with a trifle—layers of cake, rich vanilla pudding, and bananas. Because this recipe is all about the toppings, it's fine to use box cake mix—or even a store-bought cake—instead of homemade.

6 bananas

2 (3-ounce) boxes instant banana cream pudding mix, prepared according to package directions

4 cups milk

1 box yellow cake mix, prepared according to package directions and baked in two 8-inch round cake pans

½ cup strawberry sundae topping (store-bought)

2½ cups Sprinkles Whipped Cream (page 41)

½ cup pineapple sundae topping

1 cup chocolate syrup

1 maraschino cherry

¼ cup rainbow jimmies

¼ cup chopped nuts

1 Slice 2 of the bananas into ½-inch rounds and fold into prepared pudding. Cut the remaining 4 bananas into quarters.

2 Using a serrated knife, level tops of cakes and then slice each in half horizontally, making 4 thin layers. Place 1 layer in the bottom of a 4-quart trifle bowl. Spread with strawberry sundae topping, ½ cup pudding, and ¾ cup whipped cream.

3 Arrange 4 banana quarters on top; top with another cake layer. Continue layering ingredients, spreading pineapple topping on the second cake layer and half of the chocolate syrup on the third.

4 Decorate the final banana layer with a dollop of whipped cream. Drizzle with the remaining chocolate syrup; top with cherry. Decorate with jimmies and nuts. Spoon individual portions into bowls. Serve immediately.

PERSONAL PORTIONS

No need to share! Layer ingredients in parfait glasses instead of one large bowl for single-serving trifle treats.

a box of chocolates in brownie form

❖ Brownie Bites ❖

MAKES 24 MINI BROWNIES

These rich, mini-muffin-size bits of extra-gooey brownies are decorated
to look like fancy boxed chocolates. They're a great way to try out new flavor combinations and
play with the contrast of the toppings against the dark background of the bites.

1 cup all-purpose flour

3 tablespoons unsweetened cocoa powder

1 teaspoon ground coffee, optional

½ teaspoon salt

4 tablespoons (½ stick) unsalted butter, melted

1 cup sugar

⅓ cup Greek yogurt

3 eggs

1 teaspoon pure vanilla extract

½ cup mini semisweet chocolate chips

2 cups chocolate melts (page 78)* or Chocolate Buttercream (page 65)

Assorted sprinkles, such as nonpareils, dragees, flower-shaped lay-ons, whole cashews, mini candies, pop rocks, and fancy salt

*See page 78 for more on using chocolate melts.

1 Preheat oven to 350°F. Coat the wells of 2 mini muffin pans with cooking spray. Line a baking sheet with parchment paper or a silicone baking mat.

2 Whisk together flour, cocoa powder, coffee (if using), and salt in a medium bowl. Pour in melted butter and whisk until smooth.

3 In another medium bowl, whisk together sugar, yogurt, eggs, and vanilla until smooth. Add yogurt mixture to flour mixture and stir to combine. Fold in mini chocolate chips.

4 Fill wells of prepared mini muffin pans two-thirds with batter. Bake for 15 to 20 minutes, or until a toothpick inserted into the center of a brownie comes out clean.

5 Dip each brownie in chocolate melts or slather with Chocolate Buttercream and set on the lined baking sheet. Decorate with sprinkles, cocoa nibs, pop rocks, and fancy salt. Serve in colorful mini cupcake wrappers that complement the toppings.

With a personal touch, these treats make a thoughtful Mother's Day gift or birthday present. Customize your sprinkles colors for Valentine's Day or other special occasions.

a holiday classic, sprinkle-style

❖ Gingerbread Ornaments ❖

MAKES 5 DOZEN SMALL OR 3 DOZEN LARGE COOKIES

Make your little guys stand out with some sprinkle magic!

½ cup plus 2 tablespoons
unsalted butter

¾ cup sugar

½ cup light corn syrup

¼ cup milk

3 cups bread flour

1⅛ teaspoons baking soda

3¼ teaspoons ground cinnamon

2 teaspoons ground ginger

¼ teaspoon ground allspice

3 pinches ground cloves

¼ teaspoon salt

Icing and colored sugar
for decorating*

*The classic Royal Icing
recipe on page 46
works well here.*

1 Line a 9-by-9-inch baking pan with plastic wrap. In a saucepan, melt butter over medium heat. Add sugar, corn syrup, and milk and whisk continuously until the mixture's temperature reaches 100°F. Remove from heat.

2 With an electric mixer on low speed, combine bread flour, baking soda, spices, and salt. Slowly beat in butter mixture for 2 minutes, until thoroughly combined. Pour dough into pan, cover with plastic wrap, and refrigerate overnight or up to 3 days.

3 Preheat oven to 350°F. Coat several baking sheets with cooking spray or line with parchment paper. Cut chilled dough into four equal pieces.

4 On a lightly floured work surface, roll out one piece of dough and dust with more flour as needed. (Keep other dough pieces refrigerated until you're ready to use them.) Roll out dough to a thickness of ¼ inch. Using cookie cutters, cut shapes out of dough and place them about 1 inch apart on prepared sheets.

5 Bake small cookies for 10 to 12 minutes and larger cookies for 15 minutes, or until slightly brown on the edges and firm to the touch. Cool sheets on wire racks for a couple of minutes before using a metal spatula to transfer cookies onto wire racks to finish cooling.

6 Decorate cooled cookies with icing and colored sugars as desired. Store in an airtight container for up to 2 weeks; if storing decorated cookies, stack them between sheets of wax paper.

PLAN AHEAD

Chilling the dough allows the flavors meld. You can also double-wrap and freeze it for several weeks.

Cookies, Cakes, and Pies

Deck the halls! Decorate and hang Gingerbread Ornaments (page 86) and Windowpane Cookies (page 60) to spice up the holidays.

a haze of orange glaze

Orange Glaze

MAKES ABOUT 1 CUP

Add a burst of fresh, sweet citrus flavor with this citrus-infused glaze.

2½ tablespoons unsalted butter, at room temperature

1½ cups confectioners' sugar

2 tablespoons orange zest

1½ to 2 tablespoons orange juice

Beat butter and sugar with an electric mixer on medium speed for 2 to 3 minutes, or until light and fluffy. Add zest and juice and mix until smooth.

Citrus Glazes

Try lemon, grapefruit, lime, or a combination of citrus zests for a variety of flavors. Simply replace the 2 tablespoons orange zest with an equal amount of the citrus zest(s) of your choice.

bright and sparkly sweets

❖ Orange Dreamsicle Cookies ❖

MAKES 3½ DOZEN

These round little cookies are soft, chewy, and citrusy.
Shimmering sanding sugar adds a touch of glam
to the addictive orange frosting glaze.

COOKIES

2 cups all-purpose flour

½ teaspoon baking powder

½ baking soda

½ teaspoon salt

⅔ cup softened unsalted
butter or margarine

¾ cup sugar

1 egg

2 tablespoons orange zest

½ cup orange juice

TOPPING AND FROSTING

2 cups Orange Glaze
(page 89)

About ½ cup shimmering
sanding sugar in shades of
orange and tangerine

About 2 cups buttercream,
optional, for filling

1 Preheat oven to 400°F. Line baking sheets with parchment paper or silicone baking mats. Sift flour, baking powder, baking soda, and salt into a medium bowl.

2 With an electric mixer on medium speed, cream butter and sugar for 2 to 3 minutes, or until light and fluffy. Mix in egg and orange zest. Add flour mixture and orange juice in three alternating additions, starting and ending with flour.

3 Drop small teaspoonfuls of dough 2 inches apart on prepared baking sheets. Bake for 8 to 10 minutes, rotating sheets halfway through baking. Let cool for at least 30 minutes before frosting.

4 Frost cooled cookies, using a rubber spatula to spread the orange glaze. Roll in shimmering sanding sugar to coat. Let glaze set before serving or sandwiching with buttercream. Cookies can be stored in an airtight container for up to 1 week.

Turn these little gems into sandwich cookies with a layer of buttercream frosting (page 65). They're also delicious on their own.

surprise sprinkles in the crust

❖ Key Lime Pie ❖

MAKES 1 PIE

Key limes (also known as Mexican limes) are about one-quarter the size of traditional limes and have a sweeter, more intense flavor. In a pinch, regular limes can be substituted, but always use fresh juice. In this version, the graham cracker crust is flecked with green, blue, and yellow jimmies that complement the creamy yellow custard filling.

PIE FILLING
3 egg yolks

2 teaspoons key lime zest

1 (14-ounce) can sweetened condensed milk

⅔ cup freshly squeezed key lime juice* (from about 12 key limes)

CRUST
1 Sprinkles Graham Cracker Pie Crust (page 94)

TOPPING
1 tablespoon confectioners' sugar

Sprinkles Whipped Cream (page 44)

¼ cup green, blue, and yellow jimmies and pastel-colored confetti sprinkles

Bottled lime juice is not recommended for this recipe.

1 Preheat oven to 350°F. Coat a 9-inch pie pan with cooking spray.

2 Beat egg yolks and key lime zest with an electric mixer on high speed until fluffy, about 5 minutes. Slowly pour in condensed milk and continue to beat for 4 minutes more, or until thick and creamy. Reduce mixer speed to low, pour in key lime juice, and mix for another 30 seconds to combine.

3 Pour mixture into pie crust and bake for 10 to 12 minutes, until filling is just set and has a firm custardlike consistency. Remove from oven and allow pie to cool for 10 to 15 minutes.

4 Freeze pie for 15 minutes, until it is cold but not frozen. Serve with a dusting of confectioners' sugar, a dollop of Sprinkles Whipped Cream, and jimmies.

colorful on the outside

Sprinkles Graham Cracker Pie Crust

MAKES 1 9-INCH CRUST

Thanks to the sprinkles mixed in, this pretty crust will steal
the show. It's especially good with Key Lime Pie (page 92) and chocolate
cream pies, or anything else you can dream up.

1 cup graham cracker crumbs*

5 tablespoons melted butter

1 tablespoon sugar

½ cup multicolored sprinkles,
confetti, or quins

¼ cup green, blue, and yellow
jimmies

*To make crumbs, place
14 crackers in a zip-top bag,
seal it, and smash with a
mallet or rolling pin.

1 Coat a 9-inch pie pan with cooking spray. Combine crumbs, melted butter, and sugar. Whisk in jimmies, making sure they are evenly dispersed.

2 Press mixture into the bottom and up the sides of the prepared pan, forming a border around the edge. Bake until crust is set and golden, about 8 minutes. Set aside until ready to use; cover and refrigerate for up to 1 week or freeze for up to 1 month.

Sprinkles Pastry Cream

MAKES 3 CUPS

This heavenly cream is so versatile, you can use it to pipe into cupcakes or doughnuts, fill pop tarts and pies, spread onto layer cakes, and so much more.

1 cup milk
1 cup heavy cream
½ to 1 cup sugar, divided
Pinch salt
6 egg yolks
2 tablespoons cornstarch
4 tablespoons (½ stick) unsalted butter
1½ teaspoons pure vanilla extract
½ cup sprinkles, such as nonpareils or jimmies

1 Warm milk and cream in a saucepan over medium-low heat. Stir in all but 2 tablespoons of the sugar. Whisk occasionally to dissolve sugar and keep mixture from boiling. Meanwhile, in a nonreactive (not aluminum) heatproof bowl, whisk to combine egg yolks and the remaining 2 tablespoons sugar. Slowly whisk half the milk mixture into the egg mixture. Then whisk the milk-egg mixture back into the saucepan.

2 Increase heat to medium, whisk in cornstarch, and continue whisking until cream threatens to bubble and clings to the whisk. Transfer to a bowl, cover, and refrigerate for at least 3 hours before folding in sprinkles and using.

a kid favorite

⟡ Confetti Popcorn Cake ⟡

MAKES 1 CAKE

This crazy cake looks like a bunch of bags of circus treats exploded at once, were covered in marshmallow, and then got stuffed into a Bundt pan. It's the perfect vehicle for candies, sprinkles, and crushed goodies of all sorts, whether you're throwing a party or just need to use up the last of a couple different jars of sprinkles. Try topping it with a pouf of cotton candy (as on page 122).

8 cups popped popcorn*

1½ cups pretzels**

1 cup shelled, roasted peanuts, optional

2 cups M&M candies, plus more for decorating

¼ cup rainbow jimmies, plus more for decorating

1 (16-ounce) bag mini marshmallows (about 8 cups)

½ cup (1 stick) unsalted butter

This is about 2 bags of microwave popcorn, or about ⅓ cup of kernels. Discard any unpopped kernels.

**Mini pretzels can be left whole or broken into smaller pieces. Crush large pretzels.*

1 Coat a 10-inch Bundt pan with cooking spray.

2 In a large heatproof bowl, stir to combine popcorn, pretzels, peanuts, candies, and sprinkles.

3 Melt butter in a large saucepan over low heat, stirring occasionally. Add marshmallows and stir until smooth and fully incorporated. Gently pour marshmallow mixture over popcorn mixture; stir or mix with clean hands to coat.

4 Press marshmallow-coated popcorn mixture into prepared pan. Cover and let set at room temperature for at least 1 hour.

5 Run a butter knife around the sides of the pan to loosen cake. Invert pan onto a serving platter to remove cake. Cut into pieces with a large serrated bread knife.

Place large dots in a circle around the bottom of the pan, then sprinkle in 2 tablespoons of rainbow sprinkles, so that when the cake is unmolded, the extra embellishments are on top.

Snacks and Party Fare

What could be more party perfect than a host of sprinkle-tastic snacks? Put some pizzazz in your finger food with Brazilian Chocolate Truffles, Meringue Kisses, Sweetheart Party Popcorn, and Cotton Candy Sticks. And there's no need to wait for a special occasion—a quick round of Birthday Cake Martinis and Tropical Pearl Cocktails are just the thing to sweeten up any day.

rich chocolate bonbons

❖ Brazilian Chocolate Truffles ❖

MAKES 20 TO 25 BALLS

How do you say "delicious" in Portuguese? *Brigadeiro*, that's how!
These easy-to-make balls are fun to roll in chocolate jimmies.
Box them up for the perfect hostess gift.

1 (14-ounce) can sweetened condensed milk

1 tablespoon unsalted butter, plus more for greasing pan and hands

3 tablespoons unsweetened cocoa powder

½ cup chocolate sprinkles and/or rainbow jimmies

1 Coat a large shallow pan or platter with butter or cooking spray. In a large saucepan, bring condensed milk, cocoa powder, and butter to a boil, stirring constantly with a rubber spatula. Reduce heat to medium-low and cook for 15 to 20 minutes, stirring constantly until mixture thickens. It should have the consistency of thick frosting.

2 Pour mixture into prepared pan; let cool completely and become firm (you can refrigerate it to speed up the process).

3 Grease your hands with butter and shape pieces into 1- to 1½-inch balls. Roll each ball in sprinkles. Place on waxed paper and refrigerate for at least 1 hour before serving.

super-sweet stirrers

·⬧· Party Spoons ·⬧·

MAKES ABOUT 30

These party-perfect treats are a modern twist on chocolate mendicants, a centuries-old candy made of little dollops of chocolate decorated with sprinkles, nuts, fruits, and other toppings. Serve as whimsical snack-time sweets or dunk into warm drinks like hot cocoa for an extra swirl of rich chocolate flavor— and sprinkles, too!

1 pound bittersweet chocolate

1 cup sixlets, dragées, nonpareils, or other assorted sprinkles*

Go wild! Party spoons will showcase all your favorite sprinkles.

1 Line several baking sheets with parchment paper or silicone baking mats. Arrange about 30 spoons on the sheets in even rows.

2 Melt and temper chocolate. (See page 77 for a tutorial.)

3 Drop small spoonfuls of tempered chocolate into each spoon, smoothing and spreading to fill the bowls of the spoons.

4 Gently place toppings on top of chocolate. Let set for 1 hour. Store in an airtight container in a cool, dry place for up to 2 weeks.

VARIATION

White Chocolate Party Spoons: White chocolate provides a dramatic contrast for darker toppings such as cranberries, dried cherries, colored crystal sugars, dragées, and cocoa nibs.

that's the stuff!

Chocolate- and Sprinkles- Dipped Waffle Cones

MAKES 4 LARGE OR 8 SMALL WAFFLE CONES

Here's a quick and easy party trick—waffle cones decked out
in rainbow jimmies and colorful quins or dragées! Let kids
decorate their own after you've dipped them in melted chocolate.

2 cups rainbow jimmies
¼ cup quins, pearl candy beads,
and/or dragées
About 1 pound whole chocolate
or chocolate candy melts
1 tablespoon shortening*

*Shortening isn't necessary if you
temper the chocolate, as on page
77. Shortening and the process
of tempering serve the same
purpose: giving melted chocolate
that glossy, smooth sheen.*

1 Line a baking sheet with parchment or wax paper.

2 Melt chocolate in a deep bowl. Stir in shortening. Dip each
cone halfway into the melted chocolate mixture, then hold it over
the lined baking sheet with one hand. With the other hand, gently
toss sprinkles onto the cone's surface while turning it until the
cone is covered. If desired, press dragées or larger quins around
the edge to create decorative patterns.

3 Let set for 15 minutes, or until chocolate is dry and firm to
the touch.

See page 77 for foolproof melted chocolate.

sugary, salty, sticky

❖ Fleur de Sel Caramels ❖

MAKES ABOUT 50

You'd think that something with such a fancy-sounding name might be complicated to make, but in fact these sweet and savory bite-size treats are as easy to concoct as they are to devour. (Still, if you want to let your friends believe these caramels are a feat of culinary magic, your secret's safe with us.)

1 cup sugar

1 cup heavy cream

¼ cup light corn syrup

1 tablespoon unsalted butter

½ teaspoon fleur de sel, plus more for topping*

1 tablespoon pure vanilla extract

Fleur de sel (literally "flower of salt") is a hand-harvested sea salt with distinctive flavor. Look for variations that have a pink or gray tone.

1 Line an 8-by-8 inch baking pan with a piece of parchment paper long enough to hang over the edges; butter the parchment well.

2 Combine sugar and cream in a saucepan. Bring to a boil over medium-high heat, stirring constantly to prevent burning. Add corn syrup and continue cooking until the mixture's temperature reaches 230°F. Stir in butter. Continue cooking and stirring mixture until temperature reaches 245°F.

3 Remove from heat; stir in fleur de sel and vanilla. Pour mixture into pan and let cool and harden, about 3 to 4 hours.

4 Remove the caramel block from the pan and cut into squares using a sharp, well-oiled knife. Top with a few grains of fleur de sel. Stored in an airtight container in a cool, dry place, caramels will keep for up to 1 week.

CHOCOLATE-DIPPED FLEUR DE SEL CARAMELS

Melt 1 pound of chocolate (yields 2 cups melted). Temper the chocolate according to the tutorial on page 77. (Tempering will give the candies a smooth finish but is not necessary.) Dip cut caramels into the chocolate. Sprinkle a few grains of fleur de sel on top and let chocolate set for 30 minutes or until firm before serving.

party time!

⋅⁚ Birthday Cake Martini ⁚⋅

MAKES TWO 5-OUNCE COCKTAILS

Any day can be your birthday with this
decadent cake-flavored cocktail.

½ cup mini quins, sugar crystals,
or other sprinkles

½ cup white chocolate
candy melts

4 ounces cake-batter-
flavored vodka*

2 ounces orange liqueur,
such as Mandarine Napoleon
or Cointreau

¼ cup half-and-half or
vanilla ice cream

*Once a rare novelty item,
cake-batter-flavored vodka is now
available at most liquor stores.*

1 Place sprinkles in a shallow bowl that is slightly larger than the rim of the martini glass. Place candy melts in a medium heatproof bowl and microwave 1 minute, or until melted. (See page 78 for a candy melts tutorial.)

2 Dip the rim of a martini glass in melted candy, swirling to coat evenly, and then dip glass into sprinkles to coat rim. Place an additional teaspoon of sprinkles in the bottom of the glass. Let glass cool completely before proceeding—if it is warm when you fill it with the cold martini, it could crack.

3 Combine remaining ingredients in an ice-filled cocktail shaker and shake vigorously for 30 seconds. Carefully strain into the glass, being sure to avoid disturbing the candied rim.

For more cocktail rim ideas, see page 50.

Jeni's favorite sprinkles treat

❖ Dark Chocolate Peppermint ❖ Ice Cream Cones

MAKES 1

As the founder of Jeni's Splendid Ice Creams, Jeni Britton Bauer
knows a thing or two about sprinkles. She came up with
an amazing ice cream recipe just for this book! Thanks, Jeni!

2 scoops Jeni's Dark Chocolate
Peppermint Ice Cream (page 112)

1 sugar cone

Several spoonfuls white
nonpareils

1 Let ice cream soften at room temperature for 5 to 10 minutes before serving. Run a big spoon or ice cream scoop under hot water, then use it to scoop ice cream into the sugar cone.

2 Fill a small bowl with nonpareils. Turn the ice cream cone to a 45-degree angle and press it into the nonpareils to create a black-and-white look.

THE BEST SPRINKLES FOR ICE CREAM

Most people love cones covered with classic rainbow jimmies. But because their delicious crunch clashes with the smoothness of ice cream, Jeni's favorite sprinkles are tiny spherical nonpareils. Says Jeni, "They remind me of one of those great midcentury chocolate shops where the ladies behind the counter wore white gloves." Plus, "you can create an emotion with them by using one color of nonpareils and another color of ice cream." That's why she likes to cover her Dark Chocolate Peppermint ice cream with pure white nonpareils. "Somehow it makes the mint mintier and the chocolate chocolatier." Try it. I think you'll agree!

unbelievably good

The Darkest Chocolate Ice Cream in the World

MAKES 1 GENEROUS QUART

Mouth-filling, palate-gripping, intense chocolate with a fudgelike texture and a pleasingly dry finish, this ice cream is the result of Jeni Britton Bauer's career-long quest to pack as much chocolate into ice cream without taking away the ice-creaminess. It is rich, bittersweet, and dense, and the texture is slightly chewy. Folks often say it tastes like the inside of a chocolate truffle.

CHOCOLATE SYRUP

½ cup unsweetened cocoa powder

½ cup brewed coffee

½ cup sugar

1½ ounces bittersweet chocolate (55% to 70% cacao), finely chopped

ICE CREAM BASE

2 cups whole milk, divided

1 tablespoon plus 1 teaspoon cornstarch

1½ ounces (3 tablespoons) cream cheese, softened

⅛ teaspoon fine sea salt

1 cup heavy cream

½ cup sugar

2 tablespoons light corn syrup

1 For the chocolate syrup, combine cocoa powder, coffee, and sugar in a small saucepan. Bring to a boil over medium heat, stirring to dissolve sugar, and boil for 30 seconds. Remove from the heat, add chocolate, and let stand for 5 minutes. Stir until smooth. Set aside.

2 For the ice cream base, mix about 2 tablespoons of the milk with cornstarch in a small bowl to make a smooth slurry. Whisk cream cheese, warm chocolate syrup, and salt in a medium bowl until smooth. Fill a large bowl with ice and water.

3 Combine the remaining milk, cream, sugar, and corn syrup in a 4-quart saucepan, bring to a rolling boil over medium-high heat, and boil for 4 minutes. Remove from heat and gradually whisk in cornstarch slurry. Bring mixture back to a boil over medium-high heat and cook, stirring with a heatproof spatula, until slightly thickened, about 1 minute. Remove from heat.

4 Gradually whisk hot milk mixture into cream cheese mixture until smooth. Pour mixture into a 1-gallon zip-top freezer bag and submerge the sealed bag in the ice bath. Let stand, adding more ice as necessary, until cold, about 30 minutes.

5 Pour ice cream base into the frozen canister of an ice cream maker and spin until thick and creamy.

6 Pack ice cream into a storage container, press a sheet of parchment directly against the surface, and seal with an airtight lid. Freeze in the coldest part of your freezer until firm, at least 4 hours.

Always use the best ingredients available, especially when making a single-flavor ice cream. For this recipe, a high-cacao, full-bodied, fruity chocolate will cut through the cream, and the flavor will be more dramatic.

For Dark Chocolate Peppermint Ice Cream
Make the ice cream base as directed. When chilled, pour it into the frozen canister of an ice cream maker and turn on the machine. Add 4 drops of pure peppermint essential oil through the opening in the top of the machine and spin the ice cream. Process as directed.

colorful cloudlike confections

❖ Meringue Kisses ❖

MAKES ABOUT 4 DOZEN 1½-INCH KISSES

These sweet, melt-in-your-mouth pillows are studded with tiny nonpareils
in shades of white, yellow, and pink. Savor the delightful explosion of
color and crunch as you bite into their marshmallow-y centers.
Meringues are cooked at such a low temperature that the sprinkles don't melt.

About ¼ cup nonpareils in
shades of white, yellow, and pink

3 large egg whites, at room
temperature

¼ teaspoon cream of tartar

¼ teaspoon salt

½ cup sugar

½ cup confectioners' sugar

1 teaspoon pure vanilla extract

A few drops food coloring,
if desired

A few teaspoons yellow
sanding sugar

1 Preheat oven to 200°F and line 2 baking sheets with parchment paper. Use a teaspoon to place 1½-inch circles of nonpareils on sheets spaced evenly apart. The circles don't have to be perfect; you'll pipe the meringues on top.

2 In the bowl of a stand mixer fitted with the whisk attachment, beat together egg whites, cream of tartar, and salt on medium-high speed until very foamy and just barely holding a shape, about 2 minutes. In a small bowl, sift together granulated and confectioners' sugars. Gradually add sugars, continuing to beat until mixture is glossy and holds a firm shape, about 3 minutes more. Beat for 1 final minute on high speed, adding vanilla and food coloring (if using).

3 Transfer meringue to a pastry bag fitted with a large round tip and pipe onto prepared sheets, or use two spoons to form into dollops about 1½ inches in diameter. Decorate with more nonpareils and sanding sugar on top.

4 Bake until firm and crisp, about 1½ hours. Turn off oven, crack the door slightly, and let meringues cool completely in the turned-off oven, about 1 hour more.

For meringues in several colors, divide the batter into separate bowls after step 2. Add only 1 or 2 drops of a different color to each bowl, beating with a whisk to combine. (Remember, a little food coloring goes a long way!)

a bark with some bite

···❖ Chocolate Bark ❖···

MAKES ABOUT 24 2-INCH PIECES

This versatile easy-to-make candy is great for holiday gifts and afternoon snacks—
just wrap up some pieces in cellophane or little sack and add a tag or note for that special
recipient. The combination of almonds and dried cranberries is divine, but you can mix and
match any of your favorite sprinkles, nuts, dried fruits, and crushed candies.

14 ounces bittersweet chocolate
1 cup almonds, toasted
and chopped
¾ cup dried cranberries

1 Line a baking sheet with parchment paper.

2 Melt and temper chocolate (see page 77 for instructions). Pour chocolate onto the baking sheet and spread it to a thickness of about ⅜ inch.

3 Sprinkle almonds and cranberries over the chocolate, pressing them lightly so they adhere. Let set for about 1 hour.

4 Break hardened chocolate into small irregular pieces with your hands or a sharp chef's knife. Store in an airtight container in a cool, dry place for up to 1 week.

MORE TO TRY

Peppermint Bark: Temper 14 ounces white chocolate while the bittersweet chocolate sets. Pour it over the bittersweet chocolate in an even layer. Sprinkle 1½ cup crushed peppermint candies over top, pressing them lightly so they adhere. Let set for about 30 minutes. Break hardened chocolate into pieces, as in step 4.

Double Rainbow Bark: Temper 14 ounces white chocolate while the bittersweet chocolate sets. Pour it over the bittersweet chocolate in an even layer. Sprinkle ¼ cup rainbow nonpareils and ¼ cup silver dragées over top, pressing them lightly so they adhere. Let set for about 30 minutes. Break bark into pieces, as in step 4.

white chocolate, peppermint, and candy corn

⁕ Sweetheart Party Popcorn ⁕

MAKES 5 CUPS

Serve this darling treat in a gift box or tin, or whip it up
any night of the week for your favorite popcorn lover.

5 cups popped corn*

½ cup white chocolate
candy melts

1 tablespoon shortening

½ cup crushed peppermint sticks
or cinnamon candies

⅓ cup heart shaped confetti

¼ cup red cinnamon-flavored
sugar sprinkles**

*Use ⅓ cup kernels, which will
yield approximately 5 cups of
popped corn.

**I like to use Betty Crocker's
Cinnamon Sugar. The red sugar
crystals sparkle and taste like
cinnamon candy. Crushed
cinnamon candies also
work well.

1 Place popcorn in a large heatproof bowl.

2 Heat white chocolate melts in the microwave for 1 minute
or until melted. (For a tutorial, see page 78.) Stir in shortening.
Pour the mixture over popcorn and toss with a rubber spatula to
coat. Add crushed peppermint sticks or cinnamon candies, heart-
shaped sprinkles, and red cinnamon-flavored sugar sprinkles and
toss to coat.

*Mini paper party cups come in all sorts of colors and
patterns. They're perfect for portioning out popcorn party
favors before your guests arrive.*

WEEKNIGHT PARTY POPCORN

*For a simpler recipe that's just as fun, omit the peppermint
sticks, candy melts, shortening, and heart-shape sprinkles
and top popped corn with salt and sugar to taste and a
dash of nonpareils.*

glitter berry goodness

❖ Starry Night Fruit Leather ❖

MAKES ABOUT TEN 2-BY-5-INCH STRIPS

This nutritious homemade snack becomes totally
irresistible with the addition of pretty swirls of edible glitter stars.
Pack extras in lunchboxes so there's enough to share!

½ pint blueberries
1 pint strawberries
1 teaspoon pure vanilla extract
¼ cup honey
2 tablespoons edible
gold glitter stars*

*These edible gold stars come
in a tiny container, but a little go
a long way. Hold a pinch high
up in the air and let stars float
down for even distribution.*

1 Preheat oven to 150°F or lowest temperature possible. Line a baking sheet with parchment paper. Place berries in a blender and blend until liquefied. Strain through a fine-mesh sieve, discarding seeds, and pour the seedless puree back into the blender. Add vanilla and honey and blend on low speed until smooth and thoroughly combined.

2 Pour mixture onto the prepared baking sheet and spread in an even layer about ¼ inch thick. Sprinkle edible gold glitter stars over top. (Sprinkle from about 1 foot above—not too close!—for even distribution.) Place in oven 6 to 10 minutes, or until the edges pull away from the pan and the center is firm.

3 Using kitchen scissors or a pizza cutter, cut fruit leather into 2-by-5-inch strips. Store between pieces of parchment paper in plastic zip-top bags or an airtight glass container at room temperature for up to 1 week.

To make fruit roll-ups, place strips of fruit leather onto same-size strips of parchment side up. Roll up loosely and tie with ribbon or baker's twine.

sweet party favors

⋅⋅❖ Cotton Candy Pops ❖⋅⋅

MAKES 10 POPS

As a little girl, I thought cotton candy was one of the most magical things. The delicate sparkling threads are even prettier when dusted with a handful of sanding sugar, Swedish pearl sugar, heart-shaped confetti, or other sprinkles. Their small crystals cling to spun sugar better than large heavy decorations (like dragées).

10 (1½-ounce) packages (about 2 cups) store-bought cotton candy, such as Jelly Bean*

10 decorative cones, skewers, or sticks

½ cup various jimmies, confetti sprinkles and sanding sugar in a color palette to match

*Believe it or not, packaged cotton candy can be purchased at concession-supply stores and stores that sell candy. Or you can pick up a bag the next time you're at a fair or festival, saving it for party time. When sealed, it keeps for up to a year. Retailers for all-natural and bulk cotton candy are listed in the resource section.

1 To fluff packaged cotton candy, remove it from the container and unravel it by pulling off thin strips.

2 Wrap the pieces around decorative cones or sticks and then toss on edible glitter and/or party-themed sprinkles. Cotton candy can be stored in a cool, dry place for up to 2 weeks, but once decorated it should be enjoyed within 2 to 3 days.

As soon as cotton candy comes into contact with moisture, it will start to dissolve. So on a humid day, keep it packaged until right before you're ready to serve it, or wrap your Cotton Candy Pops in cellophane treat bags tied with a bow. (For cellophane treat bags, decorative ribbon, and baker's twine, see "Sprinkles Sources," page 136.)

homemade Sno-Caps

Classic Nonpareils

MAKES ABOUT 40 CHOCOLATES

Named after the teeny sprinkles used to make them, these classic confections—bittersweet chocolate drops dotted with snowy white beads—are impossible to resist. They're known by a variety of delightful names: in the United Kingdom, they're called jazzies, rainbow drops, or snowies; in Australia, they're chocolate freckles.

8 ounces bittersweet chocolate

½ teaspoon pure vegetable shortening

¼ cup white or colored sugar beads

1 Line a baking sheet with parchment paper. In a double boiler or heatproof bowl set over a pan of simmering water, melt chocolate and shortening, stirring with a rubber spatula until smooth.

2 Spoon small dollops of chocolate onto the prepared baking sheet, forming into nickel-size circles. Let cool for 20 minutes and then sprinkle with nonpareils. Let candies set in a cool place for 4 hours before serving.

Serve Classic Nonpareils and Rainbow Drops in candy dishes, tie them up in cellophane bags for gifting, or place them on frosted cakes and cookies—flat side down—for an elegant decoration.

Roy G. Biv's favorite

Rainbow Drops

MAKES ABOUT 40 CHOCOLATES

Traditional nonpareil candies are made with milk or bittersweet chocolate and dotted with white sprinkles, but both white and dark chocolate drops paired with rainbow-colored sugar beads are equally popular today.

8 ounces white chocolate or bittersweet chocolate

½ teaspoon pure vegetable shortening

¼ cup rainbow nonpareils

1 Line a baking sheet with parchment paper. In a double boiler or heatproof bowl set over a pan of simmering water, melt white chocolate and shortening, stirring with a rubber spatula until smooth.

2 Spoon small dollops of white chocolate onto prepared baking sheet, forming into nickel-size circles. Let cool for 20 minutes and then sprinkle with nonpareils. Let candies set in a cool place for 4 hours before serving.

Snacks and Party Fare

jewels of the Caribbean

⁘ Tropical Pearl Cocktails ⁘

MAKES TWO 12-OUNCE DRINKS

This drink is a variation of the Bushwacker,
a rough-sounding but sweet-tasting cocktail. I've glamorized it
by adding sprinkle bits and pearl dragées. Ahoy!

⅔ cup coconut flakes, plus more to rim glass

4 tablespoons royal blue or purple jimmies

2 ounces crème de cacao*

2 ounces white rum

2 ounces dark rum

2 ounces overproof rum, optional**

½ cup (4 ounces) coconut milk, plus more for garnish

5 to 6 cups of ice

This chocolate-flavored liqueur contains a hint of vanilla.

**Any strong rum over the typical 80 to 100 proof (40 to 50 percent alcohol by volume); 120 to 150 proof is standard for overproof rum. Skip it if you want a refreshing lightweight cocktail.*

1 Preheat oven to 325°F. Spread coconut onto a foil-lined baking sheet and toast for 3 to 5 minutes, just until golden. Let cool.

2 Combine 4 tablespoons of the toasted coconut flakes, jimmies, crème de cacao, rums, the ½ cup of coconut milk, and ice in a blender and blend until thick and smooth.

3 Place the remaining toasted coconut flakes in a shallow dish. Dip the rims of two parfait glasses in coconut milk and then dip them in toasted coconut, twirling to coat.

4 Divide drink between the rimmed glasses and drop a few pearl dragées into each. Serve with a clear straw and watch the pretty pearls ascend from the bottom of the glass as you sip.

The Bushwacker is popular on Jost Van Dyke, a Caribbean island that is said to be named after the pirate who founded it. Traditionally, the men on the island drink Painkillers (which don't contain the crème de cacao) from tin cups, whereas women sip the more ladylike Bushwackers from parfait glasses.

fresh, crisp, and sweet

❖ Mini Candy Apples ❖

MAKES 8 TO 10 APPLES

These darling little candy apples are fun for kids to make—
and amazingly easy for you to whip up when you want to create
an impressive little confection in a hurry. I like to use lady apples,
a tiny, sweet variety that resembles crab apples.

About ½ cup white candy melts*

8 to 10 small apples (such as Lady apples) with long stems

¼ cup gold sugar, silver sugar, red cinnamon-flavored sugar, and white sugar pearls, or any combination you like

Candy melts are small disks that come in a variety of colors and are available at craft stores as well as some supermarkets. For more on how to use them, see page 79.

1 Line a baking sheet with parchment paper. Place candy melts in a microwave-safe bowl on top of a plate. Microwave for 60 seconds at 50 percent power, stirring once halfway through. If candy is not completely melted, continue heating with 20-second bursts. Note: The melted candy and the bowl will be very hot, so be sure to use an oven mitt when removing it from the microwave

2 Hold apples by the stem and dip them into the hot melted candy, twirling to coat but leaving some of the fruit showing at the top. Place on the prepared sheet to cool. When all the apples are coated, place the sheet in the freezer until candy hardens, at least 15 minutes. Store in the refrigerator until ready to serve.

I love the look of white candy coating paired with red apples and white sugar pearls, but it's fun to play around and find the color combinations you like best.

MORE TO TRY

Mini Candy Pears: Double the amount of candy melts and sprinkles and swap the apples for beautiful Bosc pears.

Recipes for Homemade Sprinkles

There are so many amazing sprinkles options available for purchase, and I recommend buying them all! But there are times when homemade sprinkles are the tops. They are inexpensive to make, so they're a good choice if you want a lot of different colors or a custom color that you can't find commercially. Additionally, using homemade sprinkles is a great way to ensure that you absolutely know what's going into and onto your dessert creations, catering to sensitivities or allergies to different ingredients, colorings, or additives. These are about as pure, simple, and fun as sprinkles get.

the royal icing method

SPRINKLES

MAKES ABOUT 2 OUNCES

Jimmies are made from royal icing that has been piped out in long, thin, spaghetti-like rows onto a nonstick surface. Once the rows have dried completely, they are chopped into small pieces.

4 cups confectioners' sugar

2 egg whites*

2 tablespoons warm water

½ teaspoon pure vanilla extract

⅛ teaspoon salt

Food coloring of your choice, optional

*I like to use pasteurized egg whites, such as Just Egg Whites.

1 Line a large work surface with a sheet of wax or parchment paper. Sift confectioners' sugar into a large bowl. In a small bowl, whisk together egg whites and warm water until mixture is thoroughly combined and foamy. Whisk in vanilla extract and salt. Add egg mixture to confectioners' sugar and whisk until smooth. If needed, add more water, just ½ teaspoon at a time, until icing is very thick and smooth but still able to be piped. Fold in food coloring, if using.

2 Transfer icing to a piping bag fitted with a small round tip (usually called a #1 or #2 tip). With a steady hand, pipe long lines of icing in rows all over the papered work surface. Let icing dry completely, undisturbed, for 24 hours. (Don't cheat—for this crazy experiment to work, the icing lines must be thoroughly dried.)

3 Use a sharp chef's knife to chop dried icing into small bits. Store, refrigerated, in an airtight container for up to 2 weeks.

For chunky, rustic-looking jimmies, fit pipingbag with a wider tip.

Making your own sprinkles is 100 percent fun, super easy, and a surefire way to convince your friends you've crossed over into some domestic goddess realm they never even knew existed. It's also an excellent project for kids and a great way to learn about mixing colors. Find a good color chart and let kids figure out how to make orange or lavender or even black!

MORE TO TRY

Quins and Hearts: Use the same recipe as for jimmies, but pipe icing into dots for quins or into two connected dots to make hearts.

Chocolate Jimmies: Whisk 2 tablespoons of unsweetened cocoa powder into the confectioners' sugar in the jimmies recipe. Add a drop of brown food coloring for a darker brown hue.

Multicolored Jimmies: Divide royal icing among several bowls, tint each with a different color, and then pipe rows of several different colors of icing. Once dried, you can keep the colors separate or toss them all together for a rainbow mix.

a sweet shortcut

MARSHMALLOW FONDANT

MAKES ABOUT 2½ POUNDS

Marshmallow is tastier and easier to make than classic fondant. It can be rolled into homemade Fondant Pearls (below) or flattened and used to decorate cookies, cakes, and cupcakes.

1 (16 ounce) package mini marshmallows

2 to 4 tablespoons water

1 teaspoon corn syrup

A few drops food coloring, optional*

2 pounds (about 8 cups) confectioners' sugar

Vegetable shortening, for greasing hands and work surface

*You can also knead food coloring into small batches of the prepared fondant later, to make several different colors out of one batch.

1 Place marshmallows and water in a large heatproof bowl and microwave at 30 second intervals until melted, about 2 minutes total, stirring after each interval.

2 Stir in corn syrup and food coloring, if desired. Stir in confectioners' sugar, 1 cup at a time until all is added, or until mixture becomes too hard to mix with a spoon.

3 Grease your hands and work surface with vegetable shortening. Turn fondant out onto surface and knead in any remaining confectioners' sugar with your hands.

4 Place fondant in a large ziptop plastic bag and let it rest at room temperature for several hours or overnight. It may be stored for several weeks in the refrigerator in an airtight container. Let warm to room temperature before using.

DIY dragées

FONDANT PEARLS

MAKES ABOUT ½ CUP

Pearl dragées are much too complex to make in a home kitchen, but it's easy to get the same look with a bit of fondant and luster dust. These DIY edible pearls are as easy to make as they are affordable.

½ cup fondant (store-bought or homemade)

Pinch superfine pearl dust or luster dust

Roll fondant into tiny balls. Place them in a ziptop bag with pearl dust or luster dust and shake gently to coat.

PEARLESCENT MINI CHOCOLATE CHIPS

You can also coat chocolate chips, white chocolate chips, and mini chocolate chips (aka mini morsels). Just spray them with a little vegetable oil before shaking.

Recipes for Homemade Sprinkles

sweet and sparkly

SPRINKLES SUGARS

With alternating layers of sugar and sprinkles, Mason jars of pretty Sprinkles Sugars make a lovely gift—or a fun addition to your own pantry.

In clean jars, layer ½ cup sprinkles per 1 cup sugar. Seal and store at room temperature for up to 1 year.

For vibrant, colorful sprinkles sugars, grind sugar with flowers in a food processor for 2 minutes, or until sprinkles bits are fine and evenly distributed. Store in clean jars.

rainbowlicious sweeteners

TINTED SUGARS

Try experimenting with different types of sugars, from fine grain to rock sugar; they all dye equally well. Natural sugars that have a more beige hue look just as pretty when dyed; the colors are just a bit more subdued. You can use any amount of sugar you like. For help mixing colors, consult a color chart. These are widely available online.

Granulated, crystal, or rock sugar*
A few drops food coloring

Crystal sugar has a bigger grain size than the standard sugar you find at the supermarket. This equals more sparkle, so use this sugar for extra oomph! It can be ordered online or bought at craft stores (see "Sprinkles Sources," page 136).

1 Into separate ziptop baggies, place the amount of sugar you want to color. Add 1 drop food coloring to each bag.
2 Seal bags and massage the color into the sugar. Add another drop if the color is too light.
3 Place each colored sugar on a separate parchment-paper-lined baking sheet and let dry, about 2 hours. Break up the sugar with your hands and store in jars or baggies.

PLAN AHEAD

You will need separate baking sheets or jellyroll pans for each color, if you don't want the colors to mix together while they dry.

aromatic

FLAVORED SUGARS

Flavored sugars are usually made by steeping, rubbing, or mixing a flavored ingredient with granulated sugar.

Vanilla Sugar: Immerse 1 whole vanilla bean in a clean jar full of granulated sugar, seal jar, and let sit for 1 to 2 weeks before using.

Cinnamon Sugar: Stir to combine ½ cup sugar and 2 tablespoons cinnamon. Store in an airtight container for up to 1 year.

Herb Sugar: Immerse sprigs of fresh herbs like thyme, mint, rosemary, sage, or lavender in clean jars full of any type of sugar you like. Measurements aren't too important—just be careful not to use too much lavender. Its soapy scent can easily overpower other flavors.

Citrus Sugar: With a mortar and pestle or your hands, rub lemon, lime, or orange zest into sugar to infuse it with flavor and aroma. Alternatively, you can send sugar and citrus zest for a whirl in a food processor. The smell is divine.

the original

JORDAN ALMONDS

MAKES ABOUT 4 CUPS

Jordan almonds date back to ancient Greece and their popularity predates the fifteenth century. They're often packaged in groups of five (representing happiness, health, longevity, wealth, and fertility), but secretly I like to eat them by the handful.

2½ pounds whole blanched almonds

1 pound confectioners' sugar

3 egg whites

A few drops assorted colors of food coloring, if desired

1 Preheat oven to 350°F. Line baking sheets with silicone baking mats.

2 Spread almonds in a single layer. Toast for 8 to 10 minutes, until you can smell them. Let cool.

3 Using an electric mixer on medium speed, beat sugar and egg whites together until thick. Add food coloring, if desired. (Divide mixture between two or more bowls to tint it several different shades.) Roll and toss to coat almonds with sugar mixture. Let dry on prepared sheets. Refrigerate in an airtight container for up to 3 weeks.

science can be tasty

ROCK CANDY

MAKES 3 TO 5 STICKS

This is really a science experiment on crystal growth in simple solutions, but you don't have to tell your kids that. All they need to know is that they can grow their own rock candy in a jar. It's the candy version of the pop-culture icon Magic Rocks—remember those?

2 cups water

4 cups granulated sugar, plus extra for coating sticks

A few drops food coloring, if desired

3 to 5 wooden sticks or bamboo skewers

2 teaspoons edible glitter, if desired

Pour water into a saucepan and bring to a boil over high heat. Add sugar 1 cup at a time, stirring until it is fully dissolved and the mixture is clear. Add food coloring (if using). Pour mixture into a large clean glass jar that is taller than it is wide; let cool for a few minutes. Meanwhile, dip wooden sticks in water and roll in sugar to coat. Let them dry. Place sugar-coated sticks in the cooled liquid, using clothespins to hold them in place. Space sticks evenly apart so there is room for crystals to grow. Cover jar with aluminum foil, and store undisturbed in a cool, dark place for 2 weeks, or until sticks are covered with large sugar crystals. Discard sugar solution and dip rock candy sticks in edible glitter (if using). Let dry.

See page 51 for how to turn your rock candy creation into a sparkly cocktail garnish!

Recipes for Homemade Sprinkles

Sprinkles Sources

All the sprinkles you *need* are as close as your local grocery or baking supply store—but that doesn't mean you won't *want* to stock up on more. With so many high-quality online retailers, it's never been easier to explore the wide world of sprinkles. Here are a few of my favorite suppliers.

Albert Uster Imports

www.auiswisscatalogue.com

An excellent source for gourmet and unusual sprinkles like candied flower petals, feuilletine crunch flakes, and high-end chocolate shavings. Prices are on the steeper side, so splurge accordingly!

Bake It Pretty

www.bakeitpretty.com

This charming supplier has all sorts of sprinkles, from sugar pearls to sanding sugars to quins in every shape—plus, the store is handily organized by color, so you'll have no trouble tracking down the perfect shade for your project.

Ball Jars

www.freshpreserving.com

Rustic jars with the classic mason shape and the iconic lettering are another great way to keep your sprinkles preserved—no canning needed!

Betty Crocker

www.bettycrocker.com

Timeless as ever, Betty Crocker's line of sprinkles carries all the classics plus some more recent inventions like Cinnamon Sugar (cinnamon-flavored sugar crystals).

Cake Art

www.cakeart.com

As the name suggests, this is the ultimate source for almost any kind and color of sprinkle, plus fun add-ons like icing eyes and seasonal sugar shapes.

Candyland Crafts

www.candylandcrafts.com

In addition to their nonpareils, edible glitter, and dragées, Candyland Crafts is a great resource for every confetti shape from A to Z—conveniently alphabetized.

Confectionery House

www.confectioneryhouse.com

This is an awesome place to look for sugar pearls in a multitude of sizes—right down to the millimeter!—as well as an eye-popping selection of colorful sugars and sprinkles.

Cupcake Social

www.thecupcakesocial.com

A self-described "one-stop-shop for pretty," Cupcake Social has it all: packaging and paper products, drinkware, decorating supplies, baking cups, and a jaw-dropping array of gorgeous sprinkles, Sixlets, sugars, quins, jimmies, nonpareils, dragées, glitter, pearls and beads, and candies.

Dunwoody Booth Packaging

www.dunwoodybooth.com

A great place to find any nonedible accessories (ribbons, gift bags, boxes, Easter grass, etc.) for sprucing up your sweets.

Ftsy

www.etsy.com

The handmade marketplace is also a fantastic resource for pretty bottles, jars, and glass containers of any shape.

Fun Sweets

www.funsweets.net

Packaged cotton candy in classic colors and flavors as well as creative modern flavors like cupcake and jelly bean! Fun Sweets cotton candy is available online and at retailers like Walmart, Kroger, CVS, and Dollar Tree.

Global Sugar Art

www.globalsugarart.com

Besides offering an impressive array of sprinkles and shaped sequins, this cake-decorating supplier has a great variety of luster dusts and edible glitters for adding sheen and shimmer.

HF Coors

www.hfcoors.com

American-made dinnerware, chefsware, and more. Local to Tucson, Arizona.

Holland for You

www.hollandforyou.com

A quick web search for "hagelslag" will turn up many specialty websites carrying this (usually chocolate) Dutch variety of sprinkles, but Holland for You has a particularly good selection, with top brands De Ruijter, Venz, and Lotus as well as fair-trade options.

India Tree

www.indiatree.com

With their line of "Nature's Colors" sugars and decoratifs, India Tree provides a wonderful alternative to synthetically colored sprinkles, without compromising on color or cuteness.

Just Born Candy Company

www.peepsandcompany.com

The online outpost of the popular candy company is an easy way to pick up value-size packages of classic candies like jelly beans, Hot Tamales, and licorice bits.

Kitchen Krafts

www.kitchencrafts.com

Known as the "foodcrafter's supply catalog," Kitchen Krafts stocks not just a whole rainbow of sanding sugars, disco dusts, and edible stars but also harder-to-find decorations like sugar diamonds, roses, and daisies.

M&M's

www.mymms.com

The online outlet lets you customize your chocolate candies any way you want, with colors, text, and even personalized pictures.

Sur La Table

www.surlatable.com

The gourmet go-to has quite the respectable sprinkles section, plus tons of choices for high-end chocolates, white and brown sugars, cocoa powders, and flavored finishing salts.

Target and Wal-Mart

www.target.com and www.walmart.com

Stocked much the same as their brick-and-mortar counterparts, these websites are excellent, affordable resources for national brands of jimmies, nonpareils, and shaped sequins.

Weck Jars

www.weckjars.com

The elegant and sophisticated shape of Weck canning jars is perfect for easy, eye-catching storage on your sprinkles shelf.

Williams-Sonoma

www.williams-sonoma.com

Williams-Sonoma offers high-quality sprinkles made with natural colors derived from brightly hued foods like beets, spinach, and red cabbage (but with no vegetable flavor). It's also a good source for gourmet goodies like chocolate-covered nuts and fancy finishing salts.

Wilton

www.wilton.com

The big name in cake decorating, the Wilton online store boasts an equally big arsenal of jimmies, dusts, sequins, and confettis ready for decorating.

Stock Up on Sprinkles ⋯⦂

The beauty of sprinkles is that they're a joy to look at—even when you're not eating them. Storing your sprinkles is another fun way to get creative with all the colors and textures in your arsenal. Keep them in clear containers that show off all their shine and sparkle. Mini mason jars or glass spice jars are great, but don't stop there: look for interesting or unusual vessels, like old-timey countertop apothecary jars, or stack your shakers in a spice rack to show off a whole rainbow of bits and pieces! Other useful things to have on hand are shakers (for easy mass application) and silicone cupcake liners (pinchable and pick-up-able for your day-of *mise en place*).

Index

Acknowledgments

I have written a book! My first one! And I certainly didn't do it alone. I had a huge support team of editors, friends, family, cats, and creatives. Many thanks go to the incredible people at Quirk Books. My editor, Margaret McGuire, is truly a superhero. Designer Katie Hatz art-directed with exceptional insight and, with Alison Oliver of Sugar Design, made this book look lovely and sweet. Project editor Jane Morley worked wonders. Blair Thornburgh developed an impressively thorough taxonomy of sprinkles. I don't know what I'd do without publicity and marketing experts Nicole De Jackmo, Mari Kraske, and Eric Smith. A thousand thanks go to the styling team: Rosy Strazzeri-Fridman and Danielle Westberg. I'm honored and so thankful to ice cream queen and fellow Ohioan Jeni Britton Bauer, and to Matthew Troillett for his expert assistance. Big thanks to cocktail whisperer Warren Bobrow, Pete Amplo of Sweet Tooshie's Bakery, Maribel Cervantes of Le Bon Gâteau, Jennifer Spagenberg at Cupcake Social, Brittany Egbert at Bake It Pretty, Vallory Farrosso at Wilton, Stephanie Blieberg at Sur La Table, Gretchen Goehrend at India Tree, Melanie Hebron Sutton and Dylan Sutton, Lois Ungar, Jonathan Alpers, Patty Spies, Helen Bernard, Paula Corrette-Fay, and an amazing lady at Southwest Airlines.

Last but surely not least, I'd like to thank my cats Nova and Hawthorne for their calming presence and ability to make me laugh even when I'm under a tight deadline. A thousand thanks to my husband, Jason, for his unyielding love and support, even when faced with sprinkles in every crevice of the house.

Thank you all!

Log on to QuirkBooks.com/
Sprinkles for some sweet
behind-the-sprinkles action!

**Spread the love with our shareable
Recipe Cards**

**Read a Q&A with the author, sprinkles
aficionado Jackie Alpers**

**Pin your finished recipe photos on our
Sprinkles! Pinterest board**

Put some sparkle in your sweets!